Esther's Faith

A 30-Day Women's Devotional Based on the Book of Esther

Mary Jane Humes

Proofreading, typesetting, and cover: Sally Hanan of Inksnatcher.com

Ordering Information: Quantity sales. Special discounts are available on quantity purchases by corporations, associations, and others. For details, contact the author at hello@maryjanehumes.com.

Esther's Faith: A 30-Day Women's Devotional Based on the Book of Esther/Mary Jane Humes

ISBN:

This book is lovingly dedicated to the precious memory of my father, Roland R. Rhodes, who went home to be with his Savior in October 2003. Some of the very important things my father taught me, both by his words and by his actions, were: the importance of correct Bible doctrine, the privilege of prayer, the beauty of studying Scripture, the value of hard work, the freedom of gentle, patient teaching, and the joy of generosity.

Contents

Introduction

It has been well said that truth is stranger than fiction, and the book of Esther is a wonderful example of this. For those who enjoy a good story, with a plot consisting of palace intrigue, romance, beautiful women, a not-as-clever-as-he-thought bad guy, and a humble good guy—complete with a satisfactory ending—this book in the Bible makes for great reading. Yet there is so much more in the book of Esther than just another interesting Bible story.

Some Jewish scholars see this book as a mere novella, a work of fiction to explain the origin of the Jewish feast of Purim. Others think this story is allegorical. Those who hold either view do not accept this account as actual history. They are correct that at the present time there is no surviving historical account of either Queen Esther or some of the other characters who make up this portion of Scripture. Just because there are no other recorded historical accounts about these people does not mean this narrative is not historically true.

The Library of Alexandria was one of the most significant libraries in the ancient world, and must have included, not only the chronicles of the kings of Media and Persia, as referenced in Esther chapter 10, but other historical information from that time in history. Much of the library and wealth of historical information was accidently destroyed by Julius Caesar in 48 BC during the Roman civil war. Scrolls that may have been destroyed could have included those that contained information about Queen Esther. The writer of the book of Esther uses specific names and timeframes, which indicates this is indeed a true historical account, not a work of fiction.

The book of Esther was considered pseudepigraphic (a false book of the Bible) by some of the early church fathers, and they hesitated to include it in the canon of Scripture. This biblical book is never quoted from in any of the other books of the Bible, and it does not mention either prayer or the name of God in it. But God, Who promised to preserve His words (Psalm 12:6–7), made sure this valuable gem was preserved in holy writ. This book, like the rest of God's Word, is "profitable for doctrine, for reproof, for correction, for instruction in righteousness" (2 Timothy 3:16).

The book of Esther not only shows the beauty of God protecting His people, the Jews, in giving them a remarkable triumph over adversity, but also demonstrates to the reader the wonderful goodness of God. There is much to learn about God and the Christian life in this ancient account. My desire in this devotional is to share the wonderful story of Esther with the hope the reader will develop a closer relationship with God Himself.

In Christ,

Mary Jane Humes

DAY 1

The King

BIBLE READING: ESTHER 1:1–8

BIBLE LESSON: The book of Esther begins by introducing King Ahasuerus. "Ahasuerus" actually may have been a title rather than the personal name of the king. There are scholars who believe the king mentioned in Esther was Xerxes I "the Great" of the Persian empire, who ruled from 486 to 465 BC. Regardless, Ahasuerus in the book of Esther was a real person in history. Not only was he real, but he is also, in biblical typology, a picture of God Himself. In observing Ahasuerus, the book of Esther gives us a glimpse of the character of God.

Ahasuerus was a great king and world leader. His kingdom stretched over three continents, as the Bible records in Esther 1:1, "from India even unto Ethiopia," and was comprised of 127 provinces. He was very powerful, he was royalty, he was rich, and he was famous. And if the scholars are right, and the biblical Ahasuerus was indeed Xerxes the Great, then it is recorded that he had a terrible temper. His word was law. He literally held the power of life and death over his subjects, so it was not wise to make him angry.

The book of Esther starts with the king being in a good mood and feeling very generous. He held a great feast for his court and members of his ruling elite for 180 days. Obviously, he was generous with his time-off policy, for after those days of feasting were ended, he followed with another feast—a shorter one, which lasted only seven days for all of his subjects in his kingdom.

This lavish banquet was held at the king's palace in the capital city of Shushan, and all his subjects were invited to come, enjoy, and partake of the king's generosity. This was an occasion for great rejoicing and festivity throughout the entire city.

The ornate furnishings and vibrant colors of the elaborate decorations that graced the palace are recorded in the first chapter of Esther. It was the custom of this culture for people to eat and drink while reclining on couch-like beds.

A GUEST SPEAKS: *"The king was so good to give us this feast. I was invited, but I was afraid to go. The king is so great, and I am just a commoner. My friends said it was all freely given, there was no catch. They said the food and the wine were the best they ever had. Now the feast is over, I wish I had gone!"*

TIPS ON PLEASING THE KING: At the king's feast, his wine flowed freely, but it is noted that "none did compel." The Bible records in Psalm 104:15 that "wine maketh glad the heart of man." The king freely offered heart-gladdening wine to all of his guests, yet it was up to the individual as to how much of the king's bounty he opted to receive. There were no limits to the king's generosity. The only restrictions were the ones each guest gave himself.

This royal feast is a picture of what God offers all people. He, the Creator of this wonderful and beautiful world, generously gives life to each person to freely enjoy, whether or not he believes He exists. This lavish party called "life" is a gift from God Himself.

God is the great King. He is the Creator, and He owns all things. He is the exalted One. He is the Lawgiver since He made the natural laws of the universe. God holds the power of life and death over all His creation.

Now God graciously offers eternal life to all who will come to Him. The Bible records that all have fallen short of God's perfection, and there is none worthy to enter His holy habitation called heaven. The Bible also records in the first part of Romans 6:23 that "the wages of sin is death." This is not only physical death, but spiritual death, eternal separation from God in hell.

Heaven is so wonderful that no human is good enough to enter it. But God graciously offer to impart the sinless perfection of His Son to sinful humans in order that they, too, can enjoy heaven with Him. The last part

– 3 –

of Romans 6:23 reads "but the gift of God is eternal life through Jesus Christ our Lord."

God desires that all come to Him to enjoy heaven, and He freely offers salvation from hell, but He will not compel anyone. Like King Ahasuerus's wine, God's free gift of salvation will gladden the heart of all who partake of it, but He will not compel any to take of His free gift. It is entirely up to each individual as to whether or not he will partake of His gift.

Just as some of the people in King Ahasuerus's day did not partake of his great feast but perhaps looked on it from afar, so, too, today people do not accept God's gift of eternal life. They enjoy physical life given by their Creator, but out of fear, unbelief, or some other reason, they reject the free gift of eternal life He graciously offers.

Just as King Ahasuerus was pleased when his subjects came to his feast and took what he offered, God is pleased when we come to Him for salvation. If you want to please God, accept His free gift of eternal life—today. If you already have done so, take some time and thank Him for His great salvation through His Son, Jesus Christ.

Words from Our King

Come, eat of my bread, and drink of the wine which I have mingled. Forsake the foolish, and live; and go in the way of understanding. (Proverbs 9:5–6)

Ho, every one that thirsteth, come ye to the waters, and he that hath no money; come ye, buy, and eat; yea, come, buy wine and milk without money and without price. (Isaiah 55:1)

Come unto me, all ye that labour and are heavy laden, and I will give you rest. (Matthew 11:28)

The Lord is not slack concerning his promise, as some men count slackness; but is longsuffering to us-ward, not willing that any should perish, but that all should come to repentance. (2 Peter 3:9)

Behold, I stand at the door, and knock: if any man hear my voice, and open the door, I will come in to him, and will sup with him, and he with me. (Revelation 3:20)

DAY 2

Queen Vashti, the Former Favorite

BIBLE READING: ESTHER 1:9–15

BIBLE LESSON: King Ahasuerus had a harem of women. According to Persian law, all of the women in his harem were legally married to the king; but of all of his wives, the king favored a woman by the name of Vashti. Sometime before the events recorded in the book of Esther, Vashti won the king's heart and she became queen.

While it is unknown just how Vashti obtained her elevated position, we are told how she lost it. While the king made a great feast for all his subjects, Queen Vashti also made a similar feast for all the ladies of the palace. On the final day of the feast, while King Ahasuerus was eating and drinking with his seven chamberlains, he got the idea to show off his beautiful queen, Vashti. It is supposed the king wanted Vashti to appear before him and all his guests wearing nothing but her royal crown and a smile. But regardless of what Vashti had to wear, or lack thereof, the king sent the official summons to not one but seven of his chamberlains—Mehuman, Biztha, Harbona, Bigtha, Abagtha, Zethar, and Carcas—to escort Queen Vashti into the king's presence.

Vashti's reaction to Ahasuerus's summons was unexpected—she publicly spurned the command of her king. She returned her answer that she was not going to appear via the chamberlains. Her refusal of the king's summons was just as public as his request. The king was both embarrassed and furious. Vashti had publicly humiliated him before his seven counselors and his guests. Talk of the queen's refusal spread like wildfire throughout the palace. This act of disobedience by Vashti stripped her of her royal title, and it's quite possible the king may have had her put to death too. What happened to Vashti is unknown.

VASHTI SPEAKS: *"I thought I was expressing my independence when I refused the king. I guess I had too much wine. I thought he liked strong-willed women. At least, he seemed to in private. It only took one moment of pride and a single, stupid decision. Then I lost it all."*

TIPS ON PLEASING THE KING: The account of Vashti and then Esther shows us something very interesting about God. While God loves all of His children, some are closer to Him than others, such as Abraham, Moses, David, and Daniel. He, like King Ahasuerus, does have favorites (e.g., Isaiah 66:2; Psalm

5:12). Just as King Ahasuerus chose the queen from his collection of wives, God finds His favorites from among those who are His and who choose to obey Him.

Jesus, Himself, told His disciples before He died that they were His friends, adding the admonition "if you do whatseoever I command you" (John 15:14). While Jesus had both friends and acquaintances, His friends, just like our friends, were dearer and closer to Him than all of the other people He knew. Being a friend is enjoying the status of being a favorite; and Jesus told His disciples, and us today, just how to be a friend and not merely an acquaintance of His by simply doing what He commands.

Of the multitudes who followed Jesus when He had His earthly ministry, there were seventy who followed Him and twelve He chose to be His disciples. Of those twelve, Peter, James, and John were especially close to Him, but it was John who was our Lord's favored disciple. At least four times in his gospel narrative, John refers to himself as "the disciple whom Jesus loved."

God wants us to be His favorites. Being a favorite of God does not just happen, we have to desire it and work to make it happen. We do so by obeying His commands and living our lives to please Him. Obeying God's commands brings Him glory and draws us closer to Him.

While seeking to be God's favorite is honorable, it is not a position to be taken lightly. Being a favorite is a relationship that needs to be maintained and is not without responsibility. Queen Vashti may have thought her status was secure despite what she did or did not do, but she quickly learned it was quite the opposite.

The account of Vashti shows us the coveted position of being the king's favorite can be lost. The book of Esther, which starts with the disobedience and removal of Vashti, is a warning that being the king's favorite is not to be taken for granted: Disobey the king's commands and you are in danger of losing your position. While Vashti shows us what not to do, the actions of her successor, Esther, shows the observant reader both how to win the heart of the king and maintain the "favored" status.

Let me encourage you today to make being God's favorite a goal. Live your life to please God. The apostle Paul, certainly a favorite of God's, summed up his philosophy of life and service to God in his words "For to me to live is Christ, and to die is gain" (Philippians 1:21). With an attitude like that, how could he not be a favorite of God's? God's blessings flow to His favored ones, to those who seek to please Him in obeying His commands. Obedience to God opens up a channel of blessings from Him. To enjoy the blessings of God, seek to find favor with Him daily.

Words from Our King

The LORD spake unto Moses face to face, as a man speaketh unto his friend. (Exodus 33:11)

Whosoever shall do the will of my Father which is in heaven, the same is my brother, and sister, and mother. (Matthew 12:50)

He that hath my commandments, and keepeth them, he it is that loveth me: and he that loveth me shall be loved of my Father, and I will love him, and will manifest myself to him. (John 14:21)

Ye are my friends, if ye do whatsoever I command you. (John 15:14)

The scripture was fulfilled which saith, Abraham believed God, and it was imputed unto him for righteousness: and he was called the Friend of God. (James 2:23)

DAY 3

Memucan's Counsel

BIBLE READING: ESTHER CHAPTER 1:16–22

BIBLE LESSON: When Queen Vashti refused to come at her husband's command, and not only disobeyed him but also embarrassed him, the king was furious. Being in a rage, he was unable to think clearly. Since Vashti's refusal was publicly made known, the king turned to his seven trusted counselors for advice as to what to do with his disobedient queen. These seven counselors had the privilege of daily, face-to-face access to the king. Their names were Carshena, Shethar, Admatha, Tarshish, Meres, Marsena, and Memucan.

While it is unknown what other sort of counsel was given to the king on this subject by the trusted seven, what is recorded is the accepted answer presented by Memucan. Though others may have had ideas or suggestions, it was solely Memucan's advice that the king considered and put into practice.

Memucan said Vashti's decision in not obeying her husband was setting a terrible example to everyone in the entire 127 provinces of the kingdom. Memucan concluded that the news of Vashti's public humiliation toward the king would affect all married women, who would despise the wishes of their husbands. Marriages throughout the entire kingdom would crumble.

It was advised that Ahasuerus should permanently dismiss Vashti and begin looking for a suitable replacement. The consequences of the queen's disobedience would be an example to women throughout the entire kingdom. Just as Vashti's spurning of Ahasuerus was made public, so, too, would be her immediate removal and the search for a new queen. Then, all married women in the kingdom, regardless of their social status, would be "encouraged" to honor their husbands.

The king wasted no time in making a royal law that all the husbands in his kingdom be the rulers of their house. The next order of business was to start a search for the next queen.

CARSHENA SPEAKS: *"I thought at first that Memucan's advice to the king was a bit too strong; however, I did see his point. Our queen did set a bad example for all married women. Soon, the entire kingdom will hear what she did to the king because servants talk. I am quite sure the other chamberlains sent to fetch her will be happy to pass on this juicy tidbit of gossip rather quickly. Since the queen's actions were so public, there has to be some sort of dire, and just as public, consequence. Actually, I think Memucan is worried about his own marriage because his wife is a strong-willed*

*woman herself, and he does not want her getting any
ideas from Vashti's actions. So I reluctantly agreed with
Memucan's advice to the king."*

TIPS ON PLEASING THE KING: Whether you agree
or not with Memucan concerning his analysis of the
Vashti situation, he does have a good point. Vashti set
an example but not a good one. The king had to punish
Vashti so that her actions would neither be copied nor
praised. Vashti may have thought her snubbing of her
husband would be known only by the king and his
messengers. She had no idea her actions would be
scrutinized throughout the entire 127 provinces, much
less recorded in eternal writ!

Vashti was not a submissive woman. She did not obey
the summons of her husband, who just happened to
also be her king, and therefore, she also disobeyed a
governmental order. She was, and remains, an example
of what Christian women are not to do. We Christian
women are supposed to be submissive wives. We are
told in Scripture, in Ephesians 5:22 and in Colossians
3:18, to submit ourselves to our husbands. And if that is
not enough, we, as women, not only are commanded to
submit to our husbands but are also commanded by
God to submit to those who have the rule over us. This
has the crux of both leadership in the local church and
governmental leadership. Then, as Christians, no
matter what our gender, there is a third command—we
are to submit to God.

If you are anything like me, submission is a struggle. Maybe you have the idea of submission figured out already and do it admirably. I do hope you do. But for many intelligent, thinking-and-doing ladies, to align ourselves to do what our husbands want us to do can be difficult. And sometimes it is also hard to follow the rules of the land or of those in authority in our local church. It is hard because we have a brain and we do use it. We want to express and carry out our ideas, even when they are opposed to the commands of those God has put over us.

I learned the lesson of submission to your husband when I was very young, long before I was even thinking about marriage. A dear Christian lady, who, like all of us, had some submission-to-her-husband issues, taught me a lesson I never forgot. She said, "Whenever I submit to my husband, even when I know he is wrong, God works it out." When we are submissive to husbands, our church leaders, and our government, we are actually submitting to God Himself. When we obey God, then He, not us, is responsible for the outcome. Being submissive takes a load off of us.

And being submissive is a good testimony. In a world where rebels are praised, a woman with a submissive spirit is a rarity. But in her submission, she is showing her trust in God, and that brings glory to God.

Words from Our King

Let your light so shine before men, that they may see your good works, and glorify your Father which is in heaven. (Matthew 5:16)

Let every soul be subject unto the higher powers. For there is no power but of God: the powers that be are ordained of God. (Romans 13:1)

Wives, submit yourselves unto your own husbands, as it is fit in the Lord. (Colossians 3:18)

Obey them that have the rule over you, and submit yourselves: for they watch for your souls, as they that must give account, that they may do it with joy, and not with grief: for that is unprofitable for you. (Hebrews 13:17)

Submit yourselves to every ordinance of man for the Lord's sake. (1 Peter 2:13)

DAY 4

Mordecai and Esther

BIBLE READING: ESTHER 2:1–7

BIBLE LESSON: In Esther chapter 2, the reader is introduced to Mordecai and his orphaned cousin, Hadassah, whom we know as Esther. Mordecai was a Jew (from the tribe of Benjamin) who lived in the vicinity of Shushan, the palace. At the time of the book of Esther, the Jewish people had been in captivity from the nation of Israel for four generations, judging by the naming of Mordecai's ancestors.

Mordecai's marital status is unknown; but since no wife is mentioned, he could have been a single man, a widower, or even, perhaps, a eunuch. He may or may not have had children of his own. Whatever the case, Mordecai took parental responsibility of his young, orphaned cousin Hadassah and raised her as his own daughter.

It is certain that Mordecai thoroughly instructed young Hadassah in the ways of the Lord God of Israel. He no doubt told Hadassah stories about the land of Israel, God's people, and most of all, about the God of Israel.

While Mordecai was most certainly a devoted teacher, he quite possibly had a very attentive student in Hadassah.

Once Mordecai heard the news that the king was actively searching for a replacement for Vashti, he most likely warned Hadassah that if she was taken, she was not to reveal her true ethnic identity. Perhaps it was Mordecai who gave her the Persian name of Esther, meaning "star."

Esther's legal marriage to Ahasuerus is recorded in Esther 8:2 with the following succinct phrase, "Esther was brought also unto the king's house." Once a girl was chosen—or more aptly, in this case, captured—she was the possession of the king, part of his harem, and legally married, now one of the king's wives. She could never return home to her family, could never again walk the familiar streets of her former home, and could never be married to another. The lives of the women in the harem were permanently severed from their families and their familiar surroundings.

Esther was now a married woman out of Mordecai's reach. However, Esther treasured his teaching and admonition. The Bible records, "Esther did the commandment of Mordecai, like as when she was brought up with him" (Esther 2:20). She remembered, obeyed, and treasured the things Mordecai taught her. No doubt, the echoes of Mordecai's words and his wisdom were a comfort and guide to her in the new, exotic, and unfamiliar world of the king's harem.

ESTHER SPEAKS: *"When my cousin told me the news that the king was looking for maidens to replace Queen Vashti and warned me to be careful, I never thought I would be taken. Yet he told me how to act and what not to say in the unlikely case of my being captured. I am now a married woman, but I have not even seen my husband. Everything is so different here, and I am a bit scared. I am getting used to being called Esther, my new name. I hope I will be able to remember all Mordecai taught me and also please my new keepers."*

TIPS ON PLEASING THE KING: The lives and actions of both Mordecai and Esther are an example to us. Mordecai, the father figure, instructed the student, Hadassah. The dual ability to convey the knowledge you have, while still being humble enough to accept the role of a student, is necessary and cannot be divided. Each of us has wisdom to impart and knowledge to gain. Once we realize our dual role, we need to actively apply this knowledge to our daily Christian life.

The apostle Paul knew this principle when he encouraged the young pastor Timothy, in 2 Timothy 2:2, "And the things that thou hast heard of me among many witnesses, the same commit thou to faithful men, who shall be able to teach others also." He had taught Timothy well; but even as a pastor, Timothy was still learning, and that is why Paul wrote two letters of instruction to him. Timothy also needed to pass on what he knew to those of the next generation.

The Bible says in Titus 2:4–5 that the aged women are to specifically teach the young women. Whether or not you consider yourself to be an "aged woman," you are older than some ladies and younger than others. You have knowledge and advice you can pass on to the younger generation. You don't need to have a specific title or position to teach younger women godly topics; you just need to be willing and God-fearing yourself, and you will positively influence—teach—the younger ladies. At the same time, you may turn to a younger woman to teach you a particular skill or gain some knowledge.

You can teach younger wives and mothers far more than Bible doctrine. Sharing delicious recipes, homemaking skills, sewing tips, job opportunities, budgeting help, relationship advice, babysitting services, and other similar things are all part of your teaching younger women. Remind the younger ladies that they are serving God when they maintain a good relationship with their husband and children as they keep house every day. And you, too, are serving God by being a good example to them and teaching them what you know.

Every Christian woman can help, encourage, and teach other younger ladies in some way. And when the older ladies help the younger women, both with practical knowledge coupled with a deep love of God, the family unit will be strengthened, and, according to Titus 2:5, "the word of God be not blasphemed."

Words from Our King

My son, keep thy father's commandment, and forsake not the law of thy mother. (Proverbs 6:20)

Give instruction to a wise man, and he will be yet wiser: teach a just man, and he will increase in learning. (Proverbs 9:9)

Poverty and shame shall be to him that refuseth instruction: but he that regardeth reproof shall be honoured. (Proverbs 13:18)

Train up a child in the way he should go: and when he is old, he will not depart from it. (Proverbs 22:6)

Ye younger, submit yourselves unto the elder. Yea, all of you be subject one to another, and be clothed with humility: for God resisteth the proud, and giveth grace to the humble. (1 Peter 5:5)

DAY 5

Hegai, the Chamberlain

BIBLE READING: ESTHER 2:8–9

BIBLE LESSON: In chapter 2, Esther meets Hegai, the chamberlain. He is first introduced as Hege, but later, and more often, he is referred to as Hegai. Hegai is one of many of the king's chamberlains; perhaps he was the head keeper of the virgins. More likely than not, Hegai was a eunuch. Eunuchs were castrated male servants who watched over and protected the women in the king's harem.

Hegai's job was not only to protect and take care of the women but also to teach them the intricacies of palace etiquette and protocol, including what to do and not do in the presence of the king. These peasant maidens needed to be taught how to be royal wives—princesses —for such they were to become with the proper training, as given by Hegai and his staff.

While Hegai and his helpers did all they could to mold these young women into princesses, these women still had their own free will, and in some cases, untameable spirits. Within the confines of the royal palace, each individual maiden decided just how much she wanted to obey and to learn from Hegai.

Very quickly, Esther earned the favor of Hegai. Apparently, she tried hard to please those who were in a position of authority over her. Since she pleased the chief chamberlain, he was very kind to her and made sure she got all she needed to begin her purification process. He also appointed seven maidens to act as Esther's servants and gave all eight of them the best place in the entire house of the women.

HEGAI SPEAKS: *"I never know what to expect in my job, except for dealing with all of the drama associated with catty, young, gorgeous women. Sometimes I feel I really have my hands full. But one of the girls is different. She said her name was Esther. Other than being the most beautiful woman I have ever seen, with a flawless face and figure, she seems unaware of her beauty. She has a kind, loving, and even generous spirit, making her likable to the other girls. She treats me with the utmost respect and wants to please both me and her peers. She has such a kind spirit, and the other girls all seem to gravitate to her. I will definitely be putting in a good word to the king about this one. I wonder ... am I looking at the next queen?"*

TIPS ON PLEASING THE KING: Hegai is an illustration of the local pastor. Your pastor is the "keeper" of the local bride of Christ—your church. It is the pastor's God-given responsibility to protect, nurture, teach, and prepare Christ's bride for Him. Since God called your pastor to be an overseer of the flock of God, your pastor has a different responsibility toward God. Just as Hegai was appointed to serve the king's virgins, so it is your pastor's job to serve all of the members in your local church.

Just as Hegai taught all of the maidens how to please the earthly king, so, too, does your pastor teach the flock of God about Him. Your pastor seeks God's leading for his sermons, teaching, and counsel, which he brings to all the members and visitors in his church. God uses your pastor to speak to you, and your pastor is a gift from God to you. However, it is up to you as to how much you will accept of what your pastor gives you from God's Word. You have a free will; you do not have to go to church. You can go to church and not heed a thing you hear from the man of God. That is your choice.

Perhaps part of Hegai's job was to share with the king his opinion about the different girls. The king may have highly valued Hegai's insight about his charges. Just as Hegai reported to the king about the girls, so, too, will your pastor someday give an account to God about you. Hebrews 13:17 tells us to both obey and submit to those who have the spiritual rule over us. The reason is that those in church leadership watch for our souls, and they will give an account of us to God Himself. The verse goes on to advise that their account about us to God should be good and should be given with joy and not with grief. But if they give a grievous account, this will be unprofitable for us. Submitting to the leadership of the man of God is submission to God Himself.

Respect your pastor and the position to which God has appointed him. Do what you can to make your pastor's job easier. Thank God for your pastor, pray for your pastor, respect your pastor, help your pastor, and communicate with him. Accept his service as a gift from God to you, personally; and thank him for the position he holds in the local church.

Words from Our King

Take heed therefore unto yourselves, and to all the flock, over the which the Holy Ghost hath made you overseers, to feed the church of God. (Acts 20:28)

He gave some, apostles; and some, prophets; and some, evangelists; and some, pastors and teachers; For the perfecting of the saints, for the work of the ministry, for the edifying of the body of Christ.
(Ephesians 4:11–12)

And we beseech you, brethren, to know them which labour among you, and are over you in the Lord, and admonish you; And to esteem them very highly in love for their work's sake. (1 Thessalonians 5:12–13)

Let the elders that rule well be counted worthy of double honour, especially they who labour in the word and doctrine. (1Timothy 5:17)

Obey them that have the rule over you, and submit yourselves: for they watch for your souls, as they that must give account, that they may do it with joy, and not with grief: for that is unprofitable for you. (Hebrews 13:17)

DAY 6

Mordecai Outside, Esther Inside

BIBLE READING: ESTHER CHAPTER 2:10–11

BIBLE LESSON: Soon after Esther was taken into the palace, Mordecai became busy on the outside. Every day he walked near the palace, hoping and praying, no doubt, not for just any word on the women in general —but rather, for his Hadassah. Although she was now known as Esther, she would always be Hadassah to him. She was a married woman now, out of reach of his care, living in the court of the king and in the care of the servants of her royal husband. Although Mordecai knew she was physically safe, he was concerned about her mental, emotional, and, most importantly, her spiritual welfare.

Faithful, concerned Mordecai made his daily rounds like clockwork in front of the court of the house of the women, to see if he could glean any information, any bit of royal gossip or legitimate news. He daily paced the area, perhaps looking like any other bystander, and wondered about the welfare of Hadassah. When he was tired of walking, he found that the best place to get palace information, and perhaps even a glimpse of Esther, was at the king's gate. As a commoner, he was not allowed into the palace as were the king's more privileged subjects, so he faithfully and steadfastly remained at the gate of the palace.

Meanwhile, Princess Esther was inside the palace, learning how to conduct herself as a royal wife and being prepared to come closer to the king—into his presence.

MORDECAI SPEAKS: *"I don't know why Jehovah allowed Hadassah to be taken away from me. He blessed me with her presence and now He has removed her and placed her within the palace of a heathen king. I wonder what will happen to Hadassah. I wonder how she is coping. I can only release her into Jehovah's care; only He can help her now, as there is nothing more I can do. I hope and pray she remembers all I taught her and that she will not reveal her Jewish identity."*

TIPS ON PLEASING THE KING: Mordecai is a picture of the wise, godly Christian faced with the heartrending difficulty of not being able to help a loved one. This can happen under various circumstances: A child leaves home in rebellion, refusing to speak with their parents; all forms of communication are cut off during a storm; a spouse is absent for an extended period of time, whether because of sinful choices or due to his job; a child is in surgery for hours; a precious family member has a terminal illness; or a loved one continually turns a deaf ear to the gospel. In all these circumstances, those we love are beyond our loving words, and we can do nothing to help them physically. Even when we are facing the cold, hard reality of the death of our loved ones, we can only take comfort in our sorrow and grief in releasing them into the hands of the loving God Who both gave them life and then gave them to us.

Not being able to help our loved ones in any way is a very trying event. We have all been in that situation, and we will be there again in some way. At such times, we must remember that God gave us our loved ones. He placed us into the specific families we have. No matter how we got there, He has a purpose for both us and them. He gave us our families to love and to take care of us as much as we are able. In those times in which we cannot do or say anything to help, we can only commit those we care about so dearly into the hands of a loving God. Prayer for our families and our loved ones should not be our last resort. We should be covering those we love with our prayers daily; but we need to, even more so, in times when we cannot do anything else for them but pray. Then we must trust God to love them and take care of them for us, because He is able when we are not. Although it is hard, if not impossible, to fathom, God loves our loved ones far more than we do.

Not being able to help our loved ones the way we want to leaves us only with the powerful but invisible resource of prayer. God's communication is never cut off, and we need to utilize His provision, which is more powerful than our most gallant physical attempts. God uses people, and certainly utilizes communications of various types, when we cannot "get through" to our loved ones. When we cannot do anything to help them, this is no reflection on what God can and will do. Many times, and in many circumstances, we can do nothing else but pray. God uses our prayers of faith to move His hand, and He accomplishes far more than what we could ever do in our own strength. God delights in hearing the prayers of His people since our loved ones are His too.

Words from Our King

Naked came I out of my mother's womb, and naked shall I return thither: the LORD gave, and the LORD hath taken away; blessed be the name of the LORD. (Job 1:21)

The LORD is nigh unto all them that call upon him, to all that call upon him in truth. (Psalms 145:18)

But I say unto you, Love your enemies, bless them that curse you, do good to them that hate you, and pray for them which despitefully use you, and persecute you. (Matthew 5:44)

For I am persuaded, that neither death, nor life, nor
angels, nor principalities, nor powers, nor things
present, nor things to come, Nor height, nor depth, nor
any other creature, shall be able to separate us from the
love of God, which is in Christ Jesus our Lord.
(Romans 8:38–39)

Pray without ceasing. (1 Thessalonians 5:17)

DAY 7

Esther's Preparations

BIBLE READING: ESTHER CHAPTER 2:12–14

BIBLE LESSON: After the young women were captured and taken into the harem, they instantly became the king's wives with the status of princess. But these commoners, not accustomed to royal ways and protocol, needed to change both their bodies and their minds for their position. These beautiful commoners, as charming as they most likely had been to their own people, were not appropriate for admission into the presence of the king. So these girls were subjected to an entire year of grooming.

The Bible only briefly mentions that the purification was in two parts. First, the girls were anointed with oil of myrrh for the first six months, and for the last six months, they were immersed in sweet odors. The oil of myrrh was a way to cleanse the body from all impurities and to tone the skin, making the women clean and healthy. The first six months were all about removing the impurities and odor of the women's former life.

After their bodies were purged from impurities of their former life, they were then immersed with new, clean, royal perfumes. The last six months were filled with administering the king's scents into these women. The sweet odors the girls were immersed in were most likely exclusive to the king and were only given to those he wished.

While twelve months seems to be a very long time of preparation, one of the reasons for this long time period was to make sure none of the girls was pregnant. If they came carrying a child, it was certain to appear before it was their turn to go to the king. This time period also assured that any pregnancy that did occur after the year's time was exclusively the king's progeny.

While the status of these women changed the moment they were accepted into the harem, it took at least a year for the change to show on the outside. After a year of purification, they were the same women yet they were different, both inside and out, physically and mentally.

After the twelve months of preparation, the princesses became more like the king. They wore the clothing that showed they belonged to the king. They ate the king's food. The very pores of their skin oozed of the king's perfumes, and they began to think more to the king's liking. The overall purpose of the year of preparation was to make these women have more in common with the king—far more than when they first came into the palace. After a year's time, the king's women reflected the king, not their former lives.

ESTHER SPEAKS: *"During my year of preparation, some things about me changed but others did not. During the purification process, we were schooled in the culture of the king. We learned many things about Persian culture, including politics, religion, and history. There were many things I found very interesting; but I am so glad I had the foundation from my cousin, Mordecai, of his teaching about Jehovah God. Although I never told anyone, just as Mordecai instructed me to do; silently, I am a Jew, and I intend to stay faithful to the one true God of Israel."*

TIPS ON PLEASING THE KING: When you accept Christ as your personal Savior, it takes only a single, sincere prayer to make you properly prepared for heaven. While you are totally prepared for heaven the moment you receive Christ, now you get to pattern your life, make some changes, and become more like your Savior. He is our sinless example, and His desire for His followers is to strive every day to become more like Him.

Just as it was Esther's responsibility to accept the changes to both her body and mind, so, too, we need to learn and grow to be more like Jesus Christ every day. The Bible tells us in Romans 13:14 "Put ye on the Lord Jesus Christ, and make not provision for the flesh, to fulfil the lusts thereof."

As one pastor frequently said, "Christians aren't sinless, but they should sin less." As we continue in our Christian walk, we should be less sinful and more holy, like Jesus Christ. These changes do require work. They, unlike our salvation, are not automatic; we must consciously work daily to be like Jesus Christ. We do this by praying, reading our Bible, and attending a Bible-preaching-and-teaching church on a regular basis. When God convicts us of sin and areas in our lives we need to improve—which He will—then it is our responsibility to obey

It took Esther twelve months to become more like the king; but as Christians, maintaining a holy and less sinful life before God and others is an ongoing, daily, lifetime process—sometimes a struggle. It is a chore that began when we got saved, and it's something we must actively pursue until we are finally in heaven.

Words from Our King

All thy garments smell of myrrh, and aloes, and cassia, out of the ivory palaces, whereby they have made thee glad. (Psalm 45:8)

I will greatly rejoice in the LORD, my soul shall be joyful in my God; for he hath clothed me with the garments of salvation, he hath covered me with the robe of righteousness, as a bridegroom decketh himself with ornaments, and as a bride adorneth herself with her jewels. (Isaiah 61:10)

He answered and spake unto those that stood before him, saying, Take away the filthy garments from him. And unto him he said, Behold, I have caused thine iniquity to pass from thee, and I will clothe thee with change of raiment. (Zechariah 3:4)

Be not conformed to this world: but be ye transformed by the renewing of your mind, that ye may prove what is that good, and acceptable, and perfect, will of God. (Romans 12:2)

If any man be in Christ, he is a new creature: old things are passed away; behold, all things are become new. (2 Corinthians 5:17)

DAY 8

Esther Meets the King

BIBLE READING: ESTHER CHAPTER 2:15–16

BIBLE LESSON: After the twelve-month purification ritual, the maidens were ready to come into the king's presence. Each night, one by one, a different young woman was chosen for her night of intimacy with her husband, the king. This initial meeting and romantic rendezvous had its own preparation. If the king was not pleased with her, it was possible she would never again be in his presence. Regardless of how the king viewed a particular maiden, the day after being with the king was moving day for her. After being deflowered by the king, she would be transferred to the second house of the women, under the supervision of the eunuch Shaashgaz. There she would stay for the rest of her life, unless she was one of the king's favorites and he specifically remembered her and requested her by name.

In order to make the best impression on the king, each young woman was allowed to take with her whatever she desired into the king's presence and to keep it for her very own. This was her opportunity for an unlimited shopping spree.

While this may sound very generous, the expensive things the maidens would own paled in the face of the fact that they might never again be called into the king's presence. They would live out the rest of their natural lives in the house of the women, as just another collection to his harem. Their expensive wardrobe and jewels would then be just souvenirs—a onetime gift from an absentee husband.

Exactly where Esther was in the order of the virgins, we are not told. But when it was her turn to get ready for her night with the king, she instead asked the advice and counsel of Hegai, the king's chamberlain. She let him choose the appropriate attire for her!

The Bible gives the date of Esther's first encounter with Ahasuerus. The Vashti incident occurred in the third year of the king's reign. Four years later, Esther was taken into the presence of the king for the first time.

ESTHER SPEAKS: *"Hegai told me that within a few days, it would be my turn to be with the king. I became nervous, but I wanted to make a good impression. I saw how other women dressed. Their styles ranged from very revealing to overdone opulence, and everything in-between. Hegai had always been good to me, so I asked for his help. I told him I wanted to be arrayed in a way he* *thought would most impress the king. I asked him to choose my outfit and jewelry, and to do my hair and makeup in a way he thought the king would most like. After all, Hegai knew the king far better than I did. After all, this was all about the king, and Hegai was eager to comply. The outfit he chose was not something I would have even considered. But after he was finished with me, the result was stunningly gorgeous; I was thrilled and thankful for all of his help."*

TIPS ON PLEASING THE KING: Esther sets a good example for us Christian ladies today. Esther wanted to please the king, but she was not sure how, so she humbly asked for advice from a servant of the king. We should desire to please God, though sometimes it is hard to know just how. So taking a cue from Esther, we can and should ask for advice. Just as God placed Hegai in the perfect position to help Esther, so, too, does He have people ready and willing to help us. God wants us to please Him, and He knows that sometimes we need help. For the Christian woman desiring to please God, God has given her a husband and her pastor. For the unmarried young lady living with her parents, God provided her parents as well as her pastor. Other people God has given to help us are other church leaders and other godly women.

It is wise to seek counsel with or without your husband when faced with a daunting decision. While a married woman needs to follow the leading of her husband, there may be circumstances when the husband is not available. Perhaps she finds herself abandoned by her husband, on the verge of a divorce, or in a severely troubled marriage. Or some women privately, but wisely, seek the advice of their pastor before marrying the man they are in love with.

Other times, some couples may find themselves being called by God into full-time Christian service, and they need to make many important decisions. In such situations, it is always wise to talk to someone who has been in, or is in, such service.

Sometimes there are emotional situations that need help, such as severe depression. Sometimes it can be so bad that even a Christian may consider, attempt, and perhaps succeed in taking his or her own life. In such a case, either the hurting person and/or those who have been left behind need help and counsel from a servant of God, to know how to honor God amid severe mental anguish or tragedy.

Getting wise advice from someone who is in spiritual leadership may be a humbling act, yet it is a wise decision on our part. Seek those whom God has given you as spiritual leaders in your quest to please Him. You will be a blessing both to them and to God, since you are actively seeking to bring glory to God. And you will have better chances of succeeding in your endeavors when you heed the instruction of a sincere servant of God.

Words from Our King

Let the words of my mouth, and the meditation of my heart, be acceptable in thy sight, O LORD, my strength, and my redeemer. (Psalms 19:14)

I delight to do thy will, O my God: yea, thy law is within my heart. (Psalms 40:8)

Where no counsel is, the people fall: but in the multitude of counsellors there is safety. (Proverbs 11:14)

There is a way which seemeth right unto a man, but the end thereof are the ways of death. (Proverbs 14:12)

Without counsel purposes are disappointed: but in the multitude of counsellors they are established. (Proverbs 15:22)

DAY 9

Esther Chosen as Queen

BIBLE READING: ESTHER CHAPTER 2:17–18

BIBLE LESSON: After enjoying Esther's company for some time, the king realized she was THE ONE. Of all his many wives, this one was different, special, yes, even regal. He decided he was going to make this particular woman his new queen.

While it is not recorded what made Esther the royal favorite and eventual new queen, we can speculate. I think, personally, that Esther lavished genuine praise and thanksgiving on her husband, coupled with sincere gratitude and appreciation for him, despite her circumstances. Before her first meeting with the king, she had not seen him, even though they had been married at least a year. Despite his (to us) underhanded way of obtaining his wives, the king was good to them. He gave all his wives access to his royal bounty, whatever they needed. Esther sensed the greatness of her king and told him so. Men like, even need, genuine praise, especially from their women. Esther undoubtedly knew that and genuinely praised him just because he was her husband, not necessarily because she was vying to become queen.

Her respect and genuine admiration of him supposedly made him fall madly in love with her. When he had a bad day, he needed Esther. When he had a good day, he wanted her. His sweet, kind, Esther was so much on his mind that he had no choice but to make her queen. He knew he could trust the heart and mind of this woman not to hurt or embarrass him, as did Vashti.

To celebrate the new queen, King Ahasuerus made a great and joyful feast for his subjects. He named this "Esther's feast" in honor and praise of his new queen, and gave the gift of suspended taxes to all of the provinces. The king wanted to share his happiness with his subjects during this happy, joyful, and generous time of celebration, and so he gave lavish gifts to all well-wishers.

ESTHER SPEAKS: *"My head is spinning! I was honored the king asked for my presence in his royal chamber several times. At first, I was very nervous, but then I looked forward to being with him. As I got to know him, I discovered that despite his unfair way of looking for a wife, he was really a good man. We became friends. I started to fall in love with him. One night he told me he had decided to make me queen!"*

TIPS ON PLEASING THE KING: While it is speculation as to why Esther was chosen to be queen, there are some clues. While I believe part of her charm was that of truly heaping sincere praise upon her king, she pleased him so well that he promoted her. The position of being queen was a job to perform, and Esther had proven she was the woman for the job.

More than a year earlier, when Esther was first captured and became one of the king's legal wives, she was a good captive wife. Emphasis here is on the word "captive" far more than on "wife." During her twelve months of preparation, Esther behaved herself wisely. While there may have been issues with some of the other girls' suicide attempts, escape plans, temper tantrums, and other uncooperative and unacceptable behaviors not fitting for royal women; Esther most likely did not exhibit any rebellious actions. She pleased her keeper Hegai well, and he rewarded her in kind. Perhaps Hegai told the king his opinion about each maiden before she met the king. Perhaps Esther came highly recommended.

Esther's cooperation is a lesson for us who want to be promoted in any office in life, or even in spiritual matters. We need to accept what we've been given to do and perform our job well if we want to be promoted. In whatever job we have been given—whether it is being a wife, raising children, working as an employee, helping at church, or even doing a favor for a friend, there are some basic rules to follow: be on time, be dependable, do what is asked of you, and do not complain. Then rinse and repeat. Those who do their job well get considered, get recommended, and eventually get promoted.

God has given each of us at least one job to do. To some of us, in some parts of our lives, He has given several. During our lifetime, our jobs change. No matter what we have to do, even if it is not strictly in the spiritual sense, the tasks are still God given. When we follow Esther's example in our personal and daily work, realizing that what we do is part of our relationship with God, then we do our work to the best of our ability. And when we gladly and fully submit to Him, we thank and praise Him for all of the employment with which He has blessed us. When God sees we are faithful in a few things, He will, in His timing, make us rulers over many things.

We, too, need to take a page from the playbook of Esther and praise our God. Just as humans want to hear praise from other humans, so, too, does God desire His children, those He redeemed, to praise and thank Him. God is good all the time, and He loves when we praise and thank Him for all He has given us, even the work He has blessed us with.

Words from Our King

His lord said unto him, Well done, good and faithful servant; thou hast been faithful over a few things, I will make thee ruler over many things: enter thou into the joy of thy lord. (Matthew 25:23)

It is required in stewards, that a man be found faithful. (1 Corinthians 4:2)

Whatsoever ye do, do it heartily, as to the Lord, and not unto men. (Colossians 3:23)

By him therefore let us offer the sacrifice of praise to God continually, that is, the fruit of our lips giving thanks to his name. (Hebrews 13:15)

Who shall not fear thee, O Lord, and glorify thy name? for thou only art holy: for all nations shall come and worship before thee; for thy judgments are made manifest. (Revelation 15:4)

Whatsoever thy hand findeth to do, do it with thy might; for there is no work, nor device, nor knowledge, nor wisdom, in the grave, whither thou goest. (Ecclesiastes 9:10)

DAY 10

Queen Esther

BIBLE READING: ESTHER 2:18–20

BIBLE LESSON: In today's Bible reading, the virgins in the palace at Shushan were gathered for a second time. The purpose of this gathering is unknown. It was possibly to introduce the new queen. After Esther was declared queen, many things changed for her. But one thing that did not change was her obedience to, and honor of, her adopted father, Mordecai. As the new first lady, Queen Esther may have been expected to make a public statement that revealed her ethnic heritage. However, the king was not concerned with his new queen's former culture, as he just loved her for who she was. In all of Esther's new queenly tasks and royal duties, she carefully and successfully obeyed Mordecai's admonition to hide her ethnicity.

Although Esther was now a married woman, the influence of her adopted father did not leave her; he had taught her well. Now it was up to her to honor him as much as possible without interfering with her new role as queen.

Many things had changed for Esther; she was in a new home and in a new and exciting position. Still, Esther kept her wits and wisely obeyed Mordecai's parting instructions to not reveal her past or her people.

Although we are not told exactly why Esther continued to obey the commandment of Mordecai, we know she did. Perhaps she sensed he was always nearby, and she was determined to be loyal to him and did not want to displease him. And perhaps, for whatever reason, she, too, saw the wisdom of remaining silent about her ethnicity.

Not proclaiming her ethnic identity was a humbling act. While the king might have questioned her about her background, she may have demurely refused to go into much detail. Rather, the secrets the new queen kept may have been one of the many charms that won his heart. In the king's mind, her humility may have contrasted starkly against the former Queen Vashti's. The king liked what he saw in her, and he knew this new queen could keep a secret and would not exert brazen independence like the former queen.

The king knew this beautiful and mysterious wife of his was madly in love with him, and he with her. Whatever her past, wherever she came from did not matter. The present and the future with his lovely new queen by his side was far more important to him.

MORDECAI SPEAKS: *"I am happy my Hadassah is now queen. The little girl I raised is now an adult and a royal. She was always obedient to me, and I hope and* *pray she will remember what I told her about keeping her identity a secret. I don't want anyone to know she is Jewish. Even though she has been exalted, I hope she will stay humble and remember to pray and to worship Jehovah God. I don't understand why Jehovah allowed my Hadassah to become queen, but I bow to His will."*

TIPS ON PLEASING THE KING: The last part of verse 20 in Esther chapter 2, "Esther did the commandment of Mordecai, like as when she was brought up with him," speaks volumes of Esther's character and is a lesson to us women today. Esther shows that she was submissive to those in authority over her. She was submissive to Mordecai when she was in his house, and she was submissive to Hegai when he suggested what to wear for the king. Although we are not given the details, it is implied she was submissive also to her king/husband.

As Christians, and especially as wives, we are told by God to submit both to our husbands and to those in authority. Submission can be hard for us independent, intelligent women. But submission does not mean bondage, rather, it leads to freedom. Wives are to be submissive to their husbands. You may be thinking, *You don't know my husband,* and you are right. But the Bible does not make exceptions. As wives, we can and should communicate our ideas, desires, and plans to our husbands; and a loving husband will consider and try to please his wife. But the responsibility to make final decisions is on the husband.

I know that with some husbands and their decisions, wives really have to exercise their faith muscles! And even when our husbands, despite our good advice, make the wrong decisions, we need to submit to their leadership. When we do, we are trusting God to work things out for His glory and for our personal good. Submission to our husband, to our church leaders, and to the government is submission to God. When we do what is right by submitting to them, we are trusting God—not our husband, not our pastor, not our government, but God—to work things out for our benefit. Trusting God truly gives us freedom, because when we obey God, then the responsibly to take care of us is laid upon Him, despite what our husband decides to do.

This concept of submission can be a hard pill to swallow. It is sometimes hard to trust the husband we can see, and sometimes even harder to trust the God we cannot see. But Esther's submissive spirit and actions got her supremely elevated. Being submissive is a strong but humble action. The Bible tells us God resists the proud but gives grace to the humble. When we are in submission—first to God, and then to all He commands us to be in submission to—we are obeying God. Obedience to God brings blessings to us both in this life and in eternity.

Words from Our King

Trust in the LORD with all thine heart; and lean not unto thine own understanding. (Proverbs 3:5)

A virtuous woman is a crown to her husband: but she that maketh ashamed is as rottenness in his bones. (Proverbs 12:4)

House and riches are the inheritance of fathers: and a prudent wife is from the LORD. (Proverbs 19:14)

Favour is deceitful, and beauty is vain: but a woman that feareth the LORD, she shall be praised. (Proverbs 31:30)

Submit yourselves to every ordinance of man for the Lord's sake: whether it be to the king, as supreme. (1 Peter 2:13)

DAY 11

Assassination Plot Foiled

BIBLE READING: ESTHER CHAPTER 2:21–23

BIBLE LESSON: After Esther is established as the new queen, Mordecai was still entrenched at the king's gate. His constant presence attracted the attention of some royal person and he offered Mordecai a job with pay. Whatever the case, whether working or seemingly loafing, Mordecai could daily be found at the gate of the king. There, while trying to watch for Esther's well-being, he became privy to something more than mere palace gossip. Two of the king's trusted chamberlains, Bigthan and Teresh, were disgruntled with their employer, the king. They were organizing a coup against the king and plotting to take over the kingdom for themselves. Whatever their motive, the king "had to go"; they were planning an assassination attempt.

Either Mordecai overheard what they were planning, or they tried to take him into their confidence in order to help them. Mordecai, immediately upon getting this information, somehow got the message to Esther, knowing she would take this threat seriously. Going through the proper channels, she then passed this information on to the king and gave the credit to Mordecai—yet without revealing his relationship to her.

After proper investigation and trial, Bigthan and Teresh were found guilty and hanged for their attempted coup. Surprisingly, Mordecai, to whom Esther was careful to give the credit, seemed forgotten. The king was safe, the bad guys were executed, and Mordecai was dismissed with nothing more than a word of thanks. This entire incident was dutifully recorded in the royal records, and life in the palace continued as it had before.

Usually, a king would heap rich rewards of gifts and promotion upon the hero for saving his life. Esther was hoping for this, but Mordecai's good deed seemingly went unnoticed.

QUEEN ESTHER SPEAKS: *"I was shocked when the servant came with this news from Mordecai. This was the first contact I'd had with him since I was brought here. I was delighted to know he was nearby, yet the news in the message the chamberlain gave me from him was very disturbing. I made sure this information got to the king immediately. I am so grateful it was Mordecai who discovered the assassination plot against my husband. Mordecai saved the king's life and thereby protected the entire province. If it had not been for Mordecai, my life* *could have been in danger. After the king was dead, the scoundrels might have come after me. I am a bit disappointed, though, that my husband did not reward Mordecai for saving his life."*

TIPS ON PLEASING THE KING: Although Mordecai did not receive any real acknowledgment of his good deed, I am sure he was satisfied knowing both Esther and the king were safe. So many times in our lives, it seems no one notices the good things we do. We may not be thanked, we don't get a raise, and the payoff for a good deed appears to be next to nothing.

Yet as Christians, we need to do good deeds. Though doing good deeds will not get us into heaven, they will be a testimony of God in our lives. Doing good just because it is the right thing to do is a reflection of God's Holy Spirit. As followers of God, we are told to do good simply because it is right.

When writing to the Galatians, the apostle Paul tells both them (and us) that as we have opportunity, we are to do good to all men, especially unto them who are of the household of faith (Galatians 6:10). The "household of faith" is a reference to other Christians.

Let me encourage you to do something good for someone today, not expecting anything in return. Give of yourself, of your time, and yes, even of your money, to do something good for other Christians. Don't just tell someone, "If you need anything, just ask me." Trust me, this phrase can become very trite very fast. If you know there is a need, be proactive in helping and just do it.

One very effective way we can help others is to pray for them. We will never know until we get to heaven how God used our prayers. If we think praying is not a practical help, we are very wrong. Although we may not understand how God works when we pray, He does work. God tells us to pray for others. The apostle Paul, possibly the greatest Christian who ever lived, asked for prayer. He knew the power of prayer because he said "prayers should be made for all men" (1 Timothy 2:1). Paul got specific in the same verse, adding, "for kings, and for all that are in authority." When God puts persons on your mind, pray for them, whether you like them or not. When you hear news, pray for the people in the news. You can always pray for their salvation; and ask God to meet all of their needs, spiritual and otherwise.

Another way we can help others, especially believers, is to give to missions. While you may support your local church financially with your tithes, and your church uses some of that money to support missionaries, you can budget some of the rest of your money to support a Christian worker or organization directly.

God, who sees in secret, has promised to reward openly those who help others privately (Matthew 6:4). God will reward you, if not in this life then in heaven, as you are a private blessing by praying for others, giving, and doing as He leads you.

Words from Our King

Be kindly affectioned one to another with brotherly love; in honour preferring one another. (Romans 12:10)

Let us not be weary in well doing: for in due season we shall reap, if we faint not. (Galatians 6:9)

The Lord make you to increase and abound in love one toward another, and toward all men, even as we do toward you. (1 Thessalonians 3:12)

Brethren, be not weary in well doing.
(2 Thessalonians 3:13)

Having your conversation honest among the Gentiles: that, whereas they speak against you as evildoers, they may by your good works, which they shall behold, glorify God in the day of visitation. (1 Peter 2:12)

Day 12

Haman, the Enemy

BIBLE READING: ESTHER 3

BIBLE LESSON: At this time in the narrative, Esther was queen for about five years, yet her ethnicity as a Jewish woman was still unknown by her husband, the king. Now, a new character in the story is introduced—Haman, the Agagite. Haman maneuvered himself quite closely to the king, becoming, in a very short time, second-in-command—a position higher than the one the seven special chamberlains held. King Ahasuerus commanded his servants to do Haman reverence just as they would to the king himself.

Mordecai, a fixture at the king's gate, refused to bow to Haman or give him reverence. The book of Esther hints that Mordecai's refusal to venerate this man was because of his Jewish faith, which prohibited worship to none but God alone. Mordecai's refusal to bow before Haman incensed Haman to the point that he wanted Mordecai dead. His fury would not be satisfied until all of Mordecai's people were purged from the entire kingdom. This would ensure Haman that no other Jew would exhibit Mordecai's audacity of not reverencing him.

Haman plotted and devised a scheme for the destruction of the Jews. He and his cronies picked the perfect date for this holocaust by casting Pur. Pur was a set of objects, perhaps similar to dice, which were believed to help the user determine the luckiest day for whatever event he planned. Using Pur, the date determined for the destruction of the Jews by Haman was the thirteenth day of the twelfth month of the Persian calendar, about eleven months from the first time "the die were cast."

There was one last obstacle Haman had to overcome: he had to get the king's permission before attempting this mass genocide of the Jews. Haman approached the king with his idea. By mixing both truth and error, Haman told the king about "a certain people" which needed to be destroyed from his kingdom. Haman sweetened the deal by offering a great sum of his own money to help the army kill the Jews.

Without questioning, and obviously trusting, Haman's judgment, the king rejected the offer of Haman's money but accepted his plan to destroy "those people" who, according to Haman, were "not profitable" for the king to allow live in his empire. The king, with Haman's help and guidance, wrote, in the unalterable law of the Medes and Persians, to designate the day of destruction of those so-called "unprofitable subjects." Haman and the king then sat down to celebrate what they considered a deed well done. However, once the news got out to the people, both Jews and non-Jews alike were greatly troubled.

MORDECAI'S PERSIAN FRIEND SPEAKS: *"Mordecai is a good man, and I am happy to call him a friend. Because of his religion, he refuses to reverence Haman. I admire the stand he has taken. Now there is this order from the king that on a certain date, about eleven months in the future, all the Jews will be destroyed. The Jews are good people. I don't understand. What is going on? I don't want to see Mordecai and the other Jews destroyed."*

TIPS ON PLEASING THE KING: Mordecai obeyed God and put Him first. He worshiped God alone, not the king nor the king's second-in-command. Even though Mordecai did not reverence Haman, he had already proven he was a loyal subject. Now it seemed Mordecai's obedience to his God was going to result in the annihilation of the Jewish people in the Persian empire.

Have you ever found yourself in a similar situation? You have truly tried to put God first and obey His commands in every aspect of your life, but then something happens, and suddenly all seems dark and very bleak; there seems to be no hope in sight. Your fate appears to be sealed in an unalterable way. You feel afraid, and rightly so.

Fear is a part of human nature. We are going to face scary times in our lives. No matter how close we are to the Lord, how we strive and even succeed in serving

Him, God will allow fearful events into our lives. Just because we find ourselves afraid, it does not mean God has abandoned us. No, He still is in control, and I believe He sometimes allows scary times into our lives to cause us to depend upon Him more.

Just as parents delight to comfort their frightened child in times of distress, so does God delight in welcoming His children when they flee to Him and tell Him they are afraid. A small child finds comfort and safety in the arms and reassuring voice of his or her big, strong, and brave parent. So we—with the faith of a small, scared child—need to run to God for His comfort, support, and solution when we are afraid.

One time, when our church was closed due to events over which we had no control, and the whole congregation found itself in a rather fearful state, our pastor wrote us a letter of encouragement. He ended the short, positive letter with the comforting words, "Fear not little flock" (Luke 12:32). These four words taken from the Bible were an encouragement during troubled times.

The phrase "fear not" is found sixty-three times in the Bible. It is a comforting command because humans, no matter in what century or circumstance, are often afraid. God knows that, so He gently admonishes us not to fear. When God tells us not to fear, indirectly He is telling us He has all of the circumstances within His control. Because He is in control, He alone can tell us with confidence, "Fear not."

Words from Our King

What time I am afraid, I will trust in thee. (Psalm 56:3)

They have said, Come, and let us cut them off from being a nation; that the name of Israel may be no more in remembrance. (Psalm 83:4)

The lot is cast into the lap; but the whole disposing thereof is of the LORD. (Proverbs 16:33)

Behold, God is my salvation; I will trust, and not be afraid: for the LORD JEHOVAH is my strength and my song; he also is become my salvation. (Isaiah 12:2)

Peter and the other apostles answered and said, We ought to obey God rather than men. (Acts 5:29)

DAY 13

The Grieving Jews

BIBLE READING: ESTHER 4:1–6

BIBLE LESSON: Upon hearing the news that King Ahasuerus had signed the law giving the Jews in his province only a mere eleven months to live, Mordecai understandably became upset. Tearing his beautiful work clothes in grief, he donned the traditional garments of those in great distress and mourning—sackcloth. Sackcloth is a rough type of material similar to burlap. The Jews wore this ugly, uncomfortable clothing during times of deep grief and mourning. Then they sat in ashes, symbolizing death and the grave.

Mordecai went into the city and cried with "a loud and a bitter cry" (v. 1). He was not only announcing the news of the planned destruction of the Jews but was also encouraging the people to pray and fast, entreating God to miraculously intervene. It seems Mordecai announced the news of the king's grim law on his way to the palace gates. He realized Esther may have been unaware of this new development, and he needed to get the news to her.

Mordecai's announcement, and his admonition to pray and fast for God to deliver the Jews, was effective. Esther 4:3 tells many of the Jews followed Mordecai's example of sackcloth, ashes, fasting, and prayer.

The province got the news before Esther did. As queen, it appears Esther was not affected by the mundane schemes or political decrees her husband signed into law. It must have caused some surprise, and even alarm, when she got the news that an old Jewish man, the very one who had reported the assassination plot some time ago, was now sitting in ashes and wearing sackcloth. Perhaps her maids and chamberlains knew she was acquainted with Mordecai in her former life. Hearing the news that he was dressed as a mourner, Esther's first thought was to provide him with better clothing. When her gift of appropriate clothing was rejected, and her queenly position preventing her from going to see Mordecai herself was realized, she summoned the chamberlain, Hatach. She trusted in his discretion to find out why Mordecai was publicly grieving.

HATACH SPEAKS: *"I don't understand my queen, yet my job is to serve her. She is so good to all. Now she is very concerned about an old Jewish man who wants to wear sackcloth and sit in ashes before the king's gate. I think she knew him before she became queen, and that she cares very much about his welfare. She sent me with some decent clothing for him, but he refused it. Now she asked me to go and inquire of him as to what is going on. I did hear some rumor about a law that would have some*

*Jews killed, including this man at the gate. As unfair as
that sounds to me, I wonder why it would cause such
distress to my lady. I guess I'll soon find out."*

TIPS ON PLEASING THE KING: The way we handle
bad news shows our character. As soon as Mordecai
heard the news that he and his people were slated for
mass destruction, he sought God. In telling this piece of
disturbing news to the other Jews, he admonished them
to fast. This time of fasting must have been
accompanied by fervent pleas to God for His
deliverance. Mordecai, himself, set the example by both
fasting and wearing the traditional mourning clothes of
sackcloth.

When my father was alive and our family received bad
news, many times his first words were, "We have to
pray about this." He would pray right then and there
and commit the problem to God. Then he would go
about his business, knowing God was in control and he
had given the problem over to the only One who could
help.

Prayer to God for His help should be our first course of
action in troubling times. God is in control. He does not
want us to be fearful. He knows what is going on, and
He wants His children to trust Him. Prayer is a humble
action, because we are admitting we have a situation
we cannot handle on our own; but we know God can,
and we are asking Him to intervene on our behalf. We
also need God's wisdom and His direction.

Our second course of action may be to share our burdens with other godly men and women and seek their advice, support, help, and services. When we have asked for God's help, He may direct us to persons who can help us in our plight, by giving us their advice, support, services, etc., and by praying on our behalf. God uses people.

As a godly person, you may find yourself the recipient of bad news. When directly faced with troubling news, let me encourage you to go to God first. While you are telling Him your problems, also ask Him for direction as to where or to whom to go next for help. God has given the members of the body of Christ to help each other. Learn from what they have to offer you. Then and only then will you be better able to help others when they need help, comfort, or advice.

When something bad happens to someone you know, especially a fellow Christian, reach out to them, be a friend, pray for them, and offer a kind and encouraging word. Perhaps you can even help financially, or meet their need in another way. Let those who are hurting know you care for them and are supportive.

Words from Our King

What nation is there so great, who hath God so nigh unto them, as the LORD our God is in all things that we call upon him for? (Deuteronomy 4:7)

Call unto me, and I will answer thee, and shew thee great and mighty things, which thou knowest not. (Jeremiah 33:3)

We know that all things work together for good to them that love God, to them who are the called according to his purpose. (Romans 8:28)

Blessed be God, even the Father of our Lord Jesus Christ, the Father of mercies, and the God of all comfort; Who comforteth us in all our tribulation, that we may be able to comfort them which are in any trouble, by the comfort wherewith we ourselves are comforted of God. (2 Corinthians 1:3–4)

Bear ye one another's burdens, and so fulfil the law of Christ. (Galatians 6:2)

DAY 14

Esther's Resolve

BIBLE READING: ESTHER 4:7–17

BIBLE LESSON: Mordecai told Hatach everything—perhaps even his relationship to Esther—including news of the sum of money Haman had promised the king upon destruction of the Jews. As proof of his words, Mordecai gave Hatach a copy of the king's decree. Mordecai further asked Hatach to tell Queen Esther she needed to go to the king and request the lives of her people. Hatach faithfully went back to the queen with the request of Mordecai; however, Esther hesitated in agreeing to Mordecai's request.

Esther replied to Mordecai's request, via Hatach, that going to the king unannounced could result in her death. No one could see the king unannounced as this was against palace protocol. Unless the king welcomed his visitor by holding out his golden scepter (a small but highly ornate staff, which was the symbol of royal authority), the intruder would be immediately executed. She further explained that she had not been called to see the king for the last thirty days (v. 11). Perhaps she added that piece of information in hope that the king would soon be requesting her presence again; and therefore, she would be invited and not have to take the initiative. Perhaps she was remembering Vashti, who had lost her position for refusing to come at the king's bidding. Now Esther was asking to come into the presence of the king at risk of death.

Assuming a fatherly role—as one who would firmly instruct a child—Mordecai, through Hatach, replied emphatically to Esther's protestations, showing his faith in God by stating the Jews would surely be delivered by some means. Also, Mordecai warned Esther that if she refused to use her position as queen, she would perish along with the rest of the Jews because of being a Jew herself. He added that it was God's will she got her position so she would save her people.

Mordecai left Esther no room to refuse. The realization of why his adopted daughter was chosen to be queen was now clear to him, and he made it clear to her. Esther understood she had no choice; this was a "do or die" situation. If she did nothing, she would face certain death; but at least by going to the king, there was a slim chance the king would hold out the scepter for her. She probably had no idea how she would approach the king with the request to spare her people. She could still be killed if she did not properly phrase her request. However, Mordecai had left her no option.

Esther made up her mind to try, but she realized she needed support, specifically prayer support. She told Mordecai to request that all the Jews fast for her and said she and her maidens would fast too. She specified that the fast was to deny themselves of both food and water for three days. While it is not mentioned, fervent prayer to Jehovah God must have accompanied this strict fast.

Esther ended her message to Mordecai, via Hatach, with words of steely resolve—"If I perish, I perish." Satisfied that his adopted daughter would do what she promised, Mordecai went to the Jews to entreat them to fast and pray for three days for wisdom, direction, and success for Esther's monumental task.

My friend Dr Charles Brown said about Hatach, "I have always been impressed by the faithful work of Hatach. Without his efforts, the whole plan would have failed. He is not mentioned again, but his deeds are memorial." Hatach is an example to all of us. Being faithful in mundane, everyday tasks can have vital and far-reaching consequences.

MORDECAI SPEAKS: *"Now I understand why my adopted daughter became queen. Jehovah put her in this position to save our people. Now I must fast and pray and ask the other Jews to fast and pray also so that she will be successful."*

TIPS ON PLEASING OUR KING: While you and I probably will not have the job of saving an entire race of people slated for annihilation, we, too, are sometimes forced into a position where it is up to us, and only us, to save a situation. We have a job only we can do which is unique to our position, our person, or our place in life. Esther's example to us is twofold: Do what is asked of you, and don't be too proud to ask for help.

Wherever in life you may find yourself as you read this devotional, let this be a reminder—you are where you are in life for God's glory and His design. You are either being prepared to do a job, or you have a job to get done now.

You are important, and your everyday tasks are also important. If you shirk your God-given duties, they will be done by someone else. So be faithful in whatever task God calls you to do or in whatever position you find yourself. No matter how lowly or how exalted the situation is, do your tasks well so that you will bring glory to His name.

Esther was the only woman, the only person, in the entire kingdom, who had a chance of success. She was unique, and so are you. Your place in life is unique to you, and what you have to do is custom-made for you and you alone. No one can ever replace you. No one else has the opportunity like you to get specific heavenly rewards only you can get. While the risks are unique to you, so are the rewards. Go forward carefully, but go forward nonetheless. Like Esther and Mordecai, prepare yourself first; then do what you alone can do for the glory of God.

Words from Our King

Be not grieved, nor angry with yourselves, that ye sold me hither: for God did send me before you to preserve life. (Genesis 45:5)

God sent me before you to preserve you a posterity in the earth, and to save your lives by a great deliverance. (Genesis 45:7)

The salvation of the righteous is of the LORD: he is their strength in the time of trouble. (Psalm 37:39)

To every thing there is a season, and a time to every purpose under the heaven. (Ecclesiastes 3:1)

I heard the voice of the Lord, saying, Whom shall I send, and who will go for us? Then said I, Here am I; send me. (Isaiah 6:8)

DAY 15

Approaching the King

BIBLE READING: ESTHER 5:1–5

BIBLE LESSON: Esther had prepared herself and others had helped her. She, her maidens, Mordecai, and many of the Jews had fasted and prayed for the last three days. Depriving themselves of both food and water, they prayed for deliverance. Their only hope was their queen interceding for her people. After three days of preparation, Esther had to act. She donned her royal apparel and adorned herself to make herself presentable to her king. Then it was time for her to go into his throne room—unannounced and unbidden. No doubt she took a long, deep breath and said one final prayer, asking for Jehovah's wisdom and grace before entering the imposing doors that led into the throne room.

After opening the door, she stood waiting for the king's invitation. This was a critical time! The king was not expecting her, and his guards were trained to subdue and even kill anyone who attempted to enter his throne room without permission. The woman arrayed in regal apparel and standing in the doorway could have been an imposter dressed as the queen. Even if Esther was recognized as the queen, depending on his mood, the king could have ordered her immediate execution.

The king saw Esther and was pleased by her appearance, so much so that he welcomed her by holding out his golden scepter. Esther came forward and accepted his invitation by touching the top of his scepter. Then he spoke the most beautiful words to her by calling her both by position and name—Queen Esther. Then he promised that whatever her request was, he would grant it.

THE KING SPEAKS: *"I saw her standing in the doorway smiling at me, and I was stunned. She was so beautiful, so gorgeous. I had forgotten the magic of her presence. There she was, my queen, my wife, my Esther. She was a vision of beauty—but here, and unbidden? A rustling snapped me out of my reverie. It was the guards moving quickly to remove her. Then, one of my chamberlains, I think it was Harbona, spoke. 'Sire, it is the queen. Do you wish to welcome her?' Then I realized what I had to do. I quickly held out my scepter to her, my eyes never leaving her face as the guards stepped back quickly. She then touched my scepter with her small hand—adorned only with the ring I'd given her. All the while I wondered what was so important to Esther that would compel her to come into*

my throne room unannounced? Didn't she know how
perilous that was?"

TIPS ON PLEASING THE KING: The writer of
Hebrews 4:16 tells us, "Let us therefore come boldly
unto the throne of grace, that we may obtain mercy,
and find grace to help in time of need." This is an
invitation sent by God Himself. Nevertheless, Esther
shows us the importance of preparing ourselves first
before approaching the throne of grace. While we are
invited to "come boldly," we must first prepare
ourselves and follow heavenly protocol.

Perhaps Esther's favorite attire was not her royal robes
but rather tattered pajama bottoms coupled with an old
T-shirt, which said "Property of the King," on it. While
this outfit may have been comfortable for her, such
attire would not have been acceptable to enter the royal
throne room to request an audience with the king. She
had to change her comfortable but unacceptable
clothing into regal attire, specifically, garments that
would please the king.

We, too, need to prepare ourselves to come to God.
Remember how it was before you got saved? You heard
the gospel message, considered it, and prepared your
heart to receive Christ as your Savior.

Part of our preparation was realizing that without
Christ, we were doomed to an eternity in hell. Then,
and only then, were you prepared to repent of your
unbelief, and to ask Christ to come into your heart and
save you from hell. Now, as a Christian, you need to

have the same mindset when it comes to approaching God with your prayer requests.

To get His ear, we need to prepare ourselves and follow His protocol. We need to strive to be always in fellowship with Him, because Psalm 66:18 tells us "if we regard iniquity in our heart, God will not hear us." We cannot expect to be welcome to the throne of grace when we have shunned the commandments and the desires of the King. Only those who are striving to live their lives in accordance to His ways are invited to come boldly into His presence. When we willfully neglect His commands, we will not be welcomed.

Our need for God's mercy and grace may come at any time. Therefore, it is our responsibility to make sure that not only are we covered with the permanent garments of salvation—the basic attire—but that we have also made the daily hygienic preparation of striving to obey God and follow His commands. We need to live a life that is pleasing to Him before the need arises to go boldly into His throne room.

Let me encourage you to put some time and thought into your personal spiritual preparations before you have need of God's mercy and grace. Preparing yourself before coming to God helps to better get His attention and receive His answers.

Words from Our King

He that turneth away his ear from hearing the law,
even his prayer shall be abomination. (Proverbs 28:9)

I will greatly rejoice in the LORD, my soul shall be
joyful in my God; for he hath clothed me with the
garments of salvation, he hath covered me with the
robe of righteousness, as a bridegroom decketh himself
with ornaments, and as a bride adorneth herself with
her jewels. (Isaiah 61:10)

Be careful for nothing; but in every thing by prayer and
supplication with thanksgiving let your requests be
made known unto God. (Philippians 4:6)

Draw nigh to God, and he will draw nigh to you.
Cleanse your hands, ye sinners; and purify your hearts,
ye double minded. (James 4:8)

Casting all your care upon him; for he careth for you.
(1 Peter 5:7)

DAY 16

Eating with the Enemy

BIBLE READING: ESTHER CHAPTER 5:6–8

BIBLE LESSON: In these verses, Esther, having received the desired attention from the king and his acceptance of her appearing, is now dining with both her king and her enemy. Haman was thrilled about this special invitation to dine with the king and queen. Consequently, he was the reason for this banquet, although he was the enemy! Haman had the massacre of Mordecai and all of Esther's people, the Jews, all carefully planned. The order had been signed by the king and the date was set. Haman was impatiently awaiting the time he would rid the kingdom of Jews. But presently, though unbeknownst to him, he was seated with, and happily enjoying the hospitality of, one of his intended victims.

While I am sure Esther was a gracious hostess, I am also sure she was a bit uncomfortable eating with the enemy of her people at her intimate banquet. While the Bible does not record the details of this banquet and wine, we can only speculate. Esther's focus was directed almost entirely on her king, with very little attention given to Haman.

Esther gazed at the king and he stared back. While no words were exchanged, their eyes spoke volumes. Esther and the king most likely enjoyed the deep and intimate, unspoken communication of two lovers.

Then the king, his curiosity no doubt piqued by this special occasion, asked, "Well, Queen Esther, what would you like? Surely you have more on your mind than just this delicious lunch?" and added sincerely, "I will give you what you ask."

With her entire focus on her king, Esther hesitated and then said, "Your majesty, if you please, come to another banquet tomorrow, and at that time I will tell you my request." She also added, "And bring Haman too."

The king smiled at her, thinking to himself that he missed Esther and that it had been far too long since he had last been with her. He agreed to her request by saying, "Well in that case, we will both be at your banquet tomorrow. Haman, I am sure you need to get home before it gets too late. You must have things to do. Take the rest of the day off and I will see you tomorrow." The king now had far more interesting things on his mind than politics.

HAMAN SPEAKS: *"At first, I was thrilled I was invited to the banquet with the king and queen. The food and* *wine were great, but I was totally ignored. Neither the king nor the queen was paying any attention to me! The queen was focusing all her attention on the king. Well, once I am king, I will certainly put this woman in her place! She will pay for ignoring me! But wait. She wants us both back tomorrow for another banquet. I do believe she recognizes that I am a special and powerful man. I like that. I will accept being second place—for now."*

TIPS FOR PLEASING THE KING: When you find yourself eating with the enemy, don't forget to have the Lover of your soul there also. How many times have you eaten with an enemy? Enemies come in many different disguises. They may be a cancer diagnosis, a strained marriage, lack of finances, the heartbreak of a wayward child, the looming death of a loved one, difficulties at work, and the list goes on. So what do you do when you come face-to-face with your enemy? Your life must continue even while you are, in a sense, sharing a meal with your enemy. Esther shows us what to do—focus on your King.

When enemies are nearby, surround yourself with, and focus on, the goodness of God and His promises to you. Ask Him to take care of both you and your difficult situation. If you have trusted Him to take your eternal soul to heaven, then you can safely and surely trust Him to take care of your problems, despite all your enemies and trials in this life. Thank and praise Him for who He is, for your salvation, for His love for you, for His Word, for all of the blessings He has given you, for seeing you through this trial. And above all, thank and praise God that He is far stronger than any and all of the enemies you are facing. The book of 1 Peter is also called "the handbook of Christian suffering"; its message is a balm to a frightened and harassed believer.

Keep your eyes on God even while your enemy is figuratively at your table. Your enemy may be staring at you, but do not stare back. Rather, look to the One who is far greater than any enemy you may face, and Who will deliver you and bring you out into a far greater place. Trust God and remember His goodness, His strength, His love, and His protection. Recount His past answers to your prayers, His deliverances, and His overcoming of your enemies. Know that even this enemy, although appearing strong, evil, and out to destroy you, is no match for your Savior. Your God is there to protect you and fight your enemy for you. Look to Him for your deliverance, no matter in what form your enemy may appear. Grab hold of the promises of God, knowing He will both protect you and, ultimately, vanquish your enemies.

Words from Our King

Be strong and of a good courage, fear not, nor be afraid
of them: for the LORD thy God, he it is that doth go
with thee; he will not fail thee, nor forsake thee.
(Deuteronomy 31:6)

Joshua said unto them, Fear not, nor be dismayed, be
strong and of good courage: for thus shall the LORD do
to all your enemies against whom ye fight.
(Joshua 10:25)

Thou preparest a table before me in the presence of
mine enemies: thou anointest my head with oil; my cup
runneth over.
(Psalm 23:5)

What time I am afraid, I will trust in thee.
(Psalm 56:3)

We may boldly say, The Lord is my helper, and I will
not fear what man shall do unto me.
(Hebrews 13:6)

DAY 17

Haman's Boasting

BIBLE READING: ESTHER 5:9–14

BIBLE LESSON: While the king and Esther were left to their romantic pursuits, the narrator followed Haman out the palace door and back to his home. Haman, full of gladness, confidence, and favor from the king and even, seemingly, from the queen herself, went merrily on his way, looking forward to the next day.

Then he saw Mordecai!

The faithful Jew sitting at the palace gate refused to reverence Haman. Haman, who brought the sentence of death upon Mordecai and all of the Jews, still wanted the reverence from those he was planning to destroy. When Mordecai did not move to bow to him, this lack of action totally raised Haman's ire.

Haman threw an impromptu party to tell his family of his good news. He recounted his accomplishments; he was the father of ten handsome sons, he was promoted to the king's right hand, and just today the queen favored him and him alone at a private banquet with the king. His envious friends listened with bated breath as he recounted the details of the banquet which he had just come from. Then he paused dramatically and added, "And tomorrow, the queen wants the king and me at another banquet!"

Yet all these glories paled, because Mordecai the Jew refused to reverence him. Seeing her husband's pained expression, Haman's wife and his friends offered him a solution to his dilemma: build a 50-cubit high (about 75 feet) gallows on which to hang Mordecai. The extra high gallows was meant to make a public example of this Jew who failed to obey his wishes. Haman thought this was a wonderful idea, and he got his people to work on it right away.

ZERESH SPEAKS: *"I am thrilled to be the wife of the king's second-in-command. Haman's promotion has given me a very prosperous lifestyle. I know Haman has designs for somehow becoming king himself. The king has already agreed to allow Haman to kill all of the Jews, and so what if a single Jew dies before the rest? The king will give Haman anything he wants, so by this time tomorrow, Mordecai will be dead and Haman will be satisfied."*

TIPS ON PLEASING THE KING: Here we see a powerful, boastful, self-centered, prideful, wicked egotist who was uncontrollably affected by a lowly Jewish man. The fact that Haman's whole day could be ruined by a single, small act by Mordecai showed that Haman allowed Mordecai to control him. Although

Haman was the king's second-in-command, he was still a weak man who held a powerful position.

Let this be a lesson to us when dealing with people we do not like. When their actions anger us to the point where we are a bit out of control just thinking about them, we are allowing them to control us. And how ironic it is when it is the very ones we dislike intensely—yes, even hate—whom we allow to control us. Even while Haman plotted and planned Mordecai's ignoble execution, he allowed Mordecai's power over him.

So what do you do when you are faced with someone who makes you furious for hours or even days later? Have you ever been in such a predicament where the very thought of the person you dislike made you furious, perhaps even to the point of "seeing red?" Have you wanted to have the ability, like Haman, to gleefully plan and, hopefully, carry out that person's "public execution?" As terrible as this may be, I think most of us, if we are honest with ourselves, can answer yes. The sad truth is that your enemy is controlling you. If you are being controlled by someone you intensely dislike, you are not being controlled by the Spirit of God. This is not healthy and it is not godly, despite what they have done to you.

So what can be done? 1 Peter 2:17 tells us to "honour all men. Love the brotherhood." This is just one of several verses telling us to love those who are Christians. You don't have to like someone, but you are commanded by

God to love him or her. There is a huge difference. You don't have to be their best friend, you don't have to agree on everything or even anything, but you are to love them, have compassion on them, pray for them, and help them.

Many times I have had the privilege of being with young people from my church. I know who they count as their close friends and which people at church annoy them. Yet when we pray together during a prayer meeting, it is such a wonderful blessing for me to hear them pray for God's blessing and help with the specific requests from those individuals they may not like. This is an example of truly "loving the brotherhood."

So if a person you may not like, or worse, comes to your mind as you read this devotional today, ask God to help you to love them. Trust me, loving them is a whole lot easier than asking God to help you to like them. I speak from personal experience. Let me encourage you to ask God to provide you with opportunities to show your love to those you dislike. Then you will be the bigger person, and it will be the Holy Spirit of God controlling you, not nasty humans. Rest assured, God has promised to deal with those who have wronged us. Let God take care of them since He can do a better, and more just, job than we can.

Words from Our King

Knowest thou not this of old, since man was placed
upon earth, that the triumphing of the wicked is short,
and the joy of the hypocrite but for a moment?
(Job 20:4–5)

Boast not thyself of to morrow; for thou knowest not
what a day may bring forth. (Proverbs 21:1)

I say unto you, Love your enemies, bless them that
curse you, do good to them that hate you, and pray for
them which despitefully use you, and persecute you.
(Matthew 5:44)

If it be possible, as much as lieth in you, live peaceably
with all men. Dearly beloved, avenge not yourselves,
but rather give place unto wrath: for it is written,
Vengeance is mine; I will repay, saith the Lord.
Therefore if thine enemy hunger, feed him; if he thirst,
give him drink: for in so doing thou shalt heap coals of
fire on his head. (Romans 12:18–20)

We know him that hath said, Vengeance belongeth
unto me, I will recompense, saith the Lord. And again,
The Lord shall judge his people. (Hebrews 10:30)

DAY 18

The Sleepless King

BIBLE READING: ESTHER 6:1

BIBLE LESSON: Chapter 6 of Esther begins with a
very interesting phrase, which is, "On that night …"
The narrator wanted the reader to know this was a very
special and particular night. The king had excused
himself from being with his queen. He knew she had
something very important on her mind, but she had not
shared her thoughts with him. While we are not privy
to the romantic details that preceded "that night," it is
my opinion that Queen Esther, in her womanly, marital
way, enjoyed her king. I believe the king, in return,
basked in her loving presence.

When he finally forced himself away from her,
knowing he had to go to his house to get some sleep, he
was unable to do so. I believe his thoughts were filled
with her: she had truly captured his heart. She had
come to him, loving him, not asking for anything, just
wanting to enjoy him. Whatever she would ask for
later, he knew he could not refuse. At one time, she was
just one face out of hundreds of lovely faces; now she

became his friend and lover, and she had never given him cause for suspicion. How could a man not be mindful and trustful of such a wonderful woman?

No doubt he was wondering what was so heavy on her mind that she risked coming into his presence, inviting Haman, too. He was likely wondering what the next day would bring at the second banquet. He had thoroughly enjoyed his private time with the queen after he had dismissed Haman, no matter what was on her mind.

THE KING SPEAKS: *"Esther, Esther, Esther ... I cannot get the thoughts of my beautiful queen out of my head. She is so much in love with me and I with her. I am not at all sleepy, yet I need to get some sleep. I have much to do tomorrow. I get to eat with her again—and with Haman. Why does she include Haman? Something is on her mind and it must be business. She literally risked her life to see me. Now, instead of telling me what she wanted, all she did was love me. She put all thoughts of business away and just enjoyed me. I am truly a very lucky man."*

TIPS ON PLEASING THE KING: The sleepless king is a type of God. God does not rest nor sleep because He has us on His mind at all times, and He is in constant attendance upon His creation. God does not need sleep because He is God. The Bible records only a single time when God rested. After God created man and finished His creation, He rested for only a single day, and it is not recorded that He ever again rested. He did not rest because He was tired but rested because He ceased from his labor of creation. Colossians 1:7 tells us "And he (Christ Jesus) is before all things, and by him all things consist."

Esther's actions, which resulted in insomnia for her king, are an excellent example for Christians who are going through trials. So often during tough times in our lives, we complain. When we complain, what we are really saying is that God made a mistake. While Esther's human king did make a mistake, our God never does. But we can learn a lesson from Esther. Instead of utter despair over the situation at hand, Esther focused on the goodness of her king and praised and loved him. Our God is good, and He is good all of the time. He is good in the midst of our trials.

Trials are part of life. So often in times of trial, we go to God complaining about how unfair life is. What we are really saying is that He is unfair to allow such things to happen in our lives. However, it is God Who is in control and who allowed the trial in our lives. In a sense, He is the cause of our trials.

Esther shows us how to deal with not the trials, rather with the One who controls our dire circumstances. While she was concerned about the plight of her people, yet, for a brief time, she put that aside and just poured out her love to her king.

Applying Esther's strategy to our lives, we need to focus on giving praise to God in and through our hard times. Praising God and His goodness through our difficult circumstances shows both God and others our faith in Him. God loves to see His children exercise faith in Him, and this pleases Him. When we please our heavenly Father, we will reap His benefits and blessings.

While we, as Christians, are invited and told to come to our God with all of our cares and concerns (and He indeed loves to hear from us), there needs to be a time when we come to God just to enjoy Him, to tell Him we love Him, to worship Him, and to let Him know we trust Him. And, I believe, the best time to do this is when we are going through some deep waters.

In times of great crisis, when all we can see is darkness, know that God is a light in our darkness. When we tell God He is good despite our trials, and that we want His will, not our own—this is worship. When we tell God we trust Him, and that we know He is good despite the circumstances He has allowed—this is praise. God loves hearing praise from His children. Just as our human relationships need encouragement and praise, so, too, does our relationship with our Lord. This is even far more precious while we are experiencing a trial.

God is up all night, both in the literal night and in the dark times of your trials. Let me encourage you today to praise Him. Like Esther's king, have Him rejoice in your praise to Him, even in your time of darkest night.

Words from Our King

On the seventh day God ended his work which he had made; and he rested on the seventh day from all his work which he had made. (Genesis 2:2)

The eyes of the LORD are upon the righteous, and his ears are open unto their cry. (Psalm 34:15)

Behold, he that keepeth Israel shall neither slumber nor sleep. (Psalm 121:4)

He is before all things, and by him all things consist. (Colossians 1:17)

We love him, because he first loved us. (1 John 4:19)

DAY 19

The King's Records

BIBLE READING: ESTHER CHAPTER 6:1–10

BIBLE LESSON: The king decided that having someone read his book of records of the chronicles of palace events would be the perfect sedative.

But something caught the king's attention, further driving away any hint of his desired sleep—it was the account of the planned assassination by his former two chamberlains but foiled by a Jew named Mordecai. The king knew he owed his life to Mordecai but could not remember how he rewarded this brave and faithful subject. The king's honor was on the line. Both as king and as a grateful human being, he was obligated to show his sincere appreciation to this man. Since he had not done so in the past, he had to immediately remedy the situation.

Dawn was breaking; it was time to get to work. Although the king had not had a wink of sleep, there were urgent matters at hand. The most pressing one was to immediately give Mordecai a lavish reward for his bravery. In his haste and sleeplessness, the king could not think of a fitting reward, but he had to do something about that right away.

Happily for the king, Haman had arrived to work early with his own agenda, which also involved Mordecai. The king was glad to see his second-in-command and figured Haman would give good advice concerning the brave and loyal Mordecai. The king had trusted Haman's advice in the past, and it always seemed that Haman had the king's best interests at heart. The king quickly summoned Haman to him and, probably, without even a hasty "Good morning," asked Haman what he should do for a man he wanted to honor.

It seemed Haman did not have to think long about this. In his pride, thinking the king wanted to honor him, Haman proceeded to tell the king what he would like from him. He was precise in every detail. He told the king to clothe the person with the royal robe and the royal crown, sit him upon the royal horse, and have one of the king's men proclaim the person was being honored by the king.

The king thought this was an excellent idea and immediately told Haman to put his plan into action—for none other than Mordecai the Jew! And the king added, almost as a warning—"Let nothing fail of all that thou hast spoken."

THE SCRIBE SPEAKS: *"I was sleeping soundly when I was suddenly awakened with news the king was summoning me to his bedroom, with the unusual request I was to read to him! And I was not to read just any bedtime story but everyday events of the palace from a few years ago! So I went. It was boring, and I had to fight weariness, but the king did not seem a bit sleepy. Then I read about the assassination attempt by the two chamberlains. This got the king's attention, and he asked me if this man, Mordecai, ever was rewarded. I knew he was not, but I pretended to read further. I told the king, no. This seemed to satisfy the king, and he finally dismissed me. I hope I will be able to get a bit of rest myself tonight."*

TIPS ON PLEASING THE KING: God, like King Ahasuerus, also keeps His book of records. His books are full of seemingly mundane accounts, details about all of our daily deeds, both good and bad. Like the brave Mordecai, we do good things for the Lord, yet it may seem our good deeds are not remembered or noticed. This account in the book of Esther should bring us encouragement. God sees all, records all, and He will reward in a great way.

Let me encourage you that every sincere prayer uttered, every gospel tract given, every hospital visit, every stray cat fed, every card sent, every weary step taken in care of a loved one, every dollar given, every encouraging note and phone call, every kind act, God knows about. He has dutifully recorded all these actions in His heavenly books. Not only does He know about the deeds performed, but He Who searches the hearts and minds also knows the why of every action. Those things done to glorify God in secret will be rewarded openly.

God will not be indebted to anyone. While many times the kind things we do seemingly go unnoticed, much less unrewarded, they are recorded and will be revealed. The Bible encourages in Galatians 6:9 "And let us not be weary in well doing: for in due season we shall reap, if we faint not."

Let the fact of God's records encourage you today to keep praying, loving others, and doing acts of kindness, knowing you are truly pleasing God; and someday, He will be pleased to reward you beyond your wildest dreams.

Words from Our King

The ways of man are before the eyes of the LORD, and he pondereth all his goings. (Proverbs 5:21)

Great in counsel, and mighty in work: for thine eyes are open upon all the ways of the sons of men: to give every one according to his ways, and according to the fruit of his doings. (Jeremiah 32:19)

Knowing that whatsoever good thing any man doeth, the same shall he receive of the Lord, whether he be bond or free. (Ephesians 6:8)

For the Son of man shall come in the glory of his Father with his angels; and then he shall reward every man according to his works. (Matthew 16:27)

And I saw the dead, small and great, stand before God; and the books were opened: and another book was opened, which is the book of life: and the dead were judged out of those things which were written in the books, according to their works. (Revelation 20:12)

DAY 20

Haman Humbled

BIBLE READING: ESTHER 6:11–14

BIBLE LESSON: In this chapter, Haman suffered quite a blow to his pride. He had no choice but to obey the king's direct orders concerning Mordecai. Haman had to go to Mordecai and tell him the good news that the king was honoring him. Then he had to dress Mordecai in the royal finery, lead a royal steed through the streets of the city, and loudly proclaim words similar to these: "This is the man the king is honoring."

Haman had to obey the king's word—and do all he had suggested for himself—concerning the despised Mordecai. Perhaps, even the thoughts of the gallows he had built for Mordecai and the upcoming royal banquet could not comfort Haman during this ordeal.

The humble Mordecai, after this honoring was past, changed back into his mourning clothes and again sat at the king's gate. Just because he was honored by the king was no reason for Mordecai to rejoice. The law that was intended to kill Mordecai, Queen Esther, and all Jewish people was still in effect. Nothing had changed. The pomp he went through that morning was meaningless in light of the distress the Jewish people were facing.

Haman, his plans gone terribly wrong, ran to the safety and security of his home to hide. He was so distraught about the role he was forced into that morning that he didn't want to be seen. The Bible says he came to his house "having his head covered." Haman probably didn't want anyone to recognize him on the street and to ask about his morning venture. However, when he got home, despite his extreme humiliation, he had to face his family and friends and tell them what happened. His wife provided no consolation. She warned him that he was now beginning to fall before the people of Mordecai and the Jews, and that he would not prevail against Mordecai, regardless of his well-planned intentions.

In the midst of all of Haman's negative emotions—grief, anger, confusion, and possibly even fear—it seems there was still a bright spot. That day was Queen Esther's second banquet, and Haman's presence was both requested and expected. Haman could not bow out of this social obligation. The messengers of the king came to escort him to the palace.

ZERESH SPEAKS: *"This was such a terrible day for us, and I fear this is just the start. We saw someone dressed in the king's robes, wearing the royal crown and seated on the king's magnificent stallion, and a man leading the horse, proclaiming, "This is what is being done for the* *man whom the king desires to honor." Haman then came home crying, very upset, and had his head covered as if in mourning. He then told us about what the king had ordered him to do—and to his enemy, no less! I fear this may be just the beginning of my husband's downfall. I wish he had not been in such a hurry to build that awful gallows intended for Mordecai."*

TIPS ON PLEASING THE KING: The lesson presented in this account is pride versus humility. Haman was very proud of his position, his wealth, and his family. The humble Mordecai realized he was totally helpless; and unless Jehovah intervened, he and all his people were going to be destroyed.

Pride is an easily besetting, subtle sin that affects each one of us. As sinful human beings, we all have some sort of pride issue somewhere in our lives. Our humility is manifested when we realize God is the source of all good things that happen to us.

Without realizing it, we can be proud of our humility. This at first seems to be an oxymoron. I once read about a man who prayed, "Lord, keep me humble." He was corrected and instructed to pray the far humbler, "Lord, make me humble."

Pride is a sin that is easy to recognize in others but very difficult to see in ourselves. Pride, which is a distorted view of oneself, effectively blinds a person to the fact that he or she is prideful. Here are some indications you (or I) may have a pride issue:

It is hard to say "I'm sorry" even when you are wrong.

You think you are special, even entitled because of your money, name, looks, education, friends, address, achievements, or something else.

You do not think you struggle with pride. Others may have a pride issue, but you don't.

You harshly condemn the sins and faults of others. Secretly, or even openly, you believe you are impervious to such evil doings.

You seek and do things in order to draw attention to yourself.

It is hard to accept constructive criticism or kind correction. You will not even consider suggestions, although sometimes you do pretend to listen.

You neglect "lesser" people. The assistants, the janitors, the secretaries, the poor, the handicapped—they are below you.

Appearance is everything. Even when you feel sad or miserable on the inside, you refuse to let it show. After all, you can take care of yourself, and you don't want anyone's pity.

Pride was the downfall of Lucifer, resulting in his becoming Satan. When we are prideful, we are like him. All we possess, all our abilities, talents, and knowledge, all our successes are only because of what God has allowed us. Refusing or even forgetting to give God the glory for our blessings is pride. God knows very well how to humble the prideful. He humbled the proud Haman, and he can humble each one of us too.

Haman's downfall was a result of his pride, and it serves as a warning to us of just how dangerous the sin of pride can be. Take some time today to ask God to make you humble.

Words from Our King

I will bless them that bless thee, and curse him that curseth thee: and in thee shall all families of the earth be blessed. (Genesis 12:2)

The afflicted people thou wilt save: but thine eyes are upon the haughty, that thou mayest bring them down. (2 Samuel 22:28)

Pride goeth before destruction, and an haughty spirit before a fall. (Proverbs 16:18)

Proud and haughty scorner is his name, who dealeth in proud wrath. (Proverbs 21:24)

I have seen servants upon horses, and princes walking as servants upon the earth. (Ecclesiastes 10:7)

DAY 21

The Second Banquet

BIBLE READING: ESTHER 7:1–6

BIBLE LESSON: The king and Haman arrived at Esther's second banquet, and while Ahasuerus had not slept the night before, he was not going to shun this get-together. He was also curious to know what Esther wanted. Alternately, Haman had experienced a very grievous morning. The dire warnings of his wife and his advisors were a niggling worry in the back of his mind. However, he alone was honored to eat with both the king and the queen a second time.

Again, the food and wine were delicious. And, like yesterday, the queen slighted Haman in favor of the king. However, Haman put that out of his mind and listened as the king asked the queen what she wanted. Haman, too, was curious.

To his astonished ears, Haman heard the queen politely and calmly plead to the king for both her life and the lives of her people. Haman was shocked. He could not believe what he was hearing. Was the queen a Jewess?

The king, too, was astonished at Esther's words. He asked, "Who would dare presume to lay hands on my queen and her people?" Then the queen firmly told the king, "The adversary and enemy ..." Here was a dramatic pause. Her voice then rose in pitch and intensity as she shouted, "is this wicked Haman!"

Then, in a flash of revelation, it seemed all of the puzzle pieces came together in the king's mind. He remembered Haman said there existed a people in his kingdom who would be in the king's best interest to be considered for complete annihilation. Trusting Haman's judgment, he remembered that he had signed the law allowing these people to be eliminated.

As the king realized what Haman had tricked him into doing, the expression on his face changed from shock to anger, and his wrathful gaze focused on his second-in-command. Haman, realizing what he had inadvertently done because of his intense hatred for Mordecai and, seeing the fury in his boss's face, became very frightened. His day was not going nearly as well as he had planned just the night before.

A ROYAL SERVANT SPEAKS: *"I heard Queen Esther, forcefully telling the king that her people were to be destroyed because of Haman. I always thought he was evil; he was never decent to us servants, and now he wants all of the queen's people destroyed. I hope the king* *finally realizes what a despicable person Haman really is."*

TIPS ON PLEASING THE KING: Esther had the ear of the king because she first had his heart. She sought his favor as a person, as a man, and as a husband. Because she was interested in him, he was receptive to anything she had to say. This is an example to the Christian today. We may have Jesus in our hearts, and that is good, very good. However, do we have His heart? That is, do we strive to please Him in all we do just because of who He is and what He means to us? When we sincerely love God for who He is and for what He has done for us, and we seek to please Him in all we do, then we truly have the heart of the King.

God loves all of His children equally (Romans 2:11), but those who are trying to please Him, trying to serve Him, concerned about His work—they are extra special to God. He pays more attention to Christians who put Him first in their lives. This passage in Esther shows that God does have His favorites. This is seen in the biblical example of the prodigal son as related in Luke 15:11–32. The father loved both of his sons very much. When the prodigal son came home to his father, the father gave him a robe, a ring, and a party. However, the older son, who consistently pleased his father, had everything. While both sons had their father's love, only the older son had all of the material goods. The older son owned the whole jewelry box, all of the clothing, and the farm itself. It appears that after the party was over, the former prodigal son, despite the deep love his father had for him, was reduced to the position of a hired servant, which consisted of a job, room, and board.

When we, as Christians, not only present our desires before God but sincerely add, "Thy will be done," and tell God that despite what we want, we desire that Christ be lifted up and that He be glorified, then we are on the way to truly pleasing God and obtaining His favor. When we want to glorify Christ and serve Him because of all He has blessed us with, God is more likely to pay attention to our prayers.

Serving God has its benefits. God honors those who honor Him, and this is shown in Esther. Esther became the favorite of the king because she sought to please him. She gave us a pattern to follow, if we desire to become a favorite of God. James 4:9 gives us a formula: "Draw nigh to God, and he will draw nigh to you." You have God's love. Now it is your choice as to whether you will desire and strive to be one of His favorites. Seeking to please God is done by drawing close to Him, obeying His commands, and seeking to magnify Christ. When we move closer to Him, He moves closer to us and is more attentive to our supplications.

Words from Our King

He will fulfil the desire of them that fear him: he also will hear their cry and will save them. (Psalm 145:19)

Call unto me, and I will answer thee, and shew thee great and mighty things, which thou knowest not. (Jeremiah 33:3)

He said unto him, Son, thou art ever with me, and all that I have is thine. (Luke 15:31)

Hitherto have ye asked nothing in my name: ask, and ye shall receive, that your joy may be full. (John 16:24)

Whatsoever we ask, we receive of him, because we keep his commandments, and do those things that are pleasing in his sight. (I John 3:22)

DAY 22

The Queen Protected

BIBLE READING: ESTHER 7:7–9

BIBLE LESSON: The scales dropped from the king's eyes, and he saw the cunning of the man he had trusted and exalted to second-in-command. Haman had tricked the king into signing the unalterable law of the Medes and Persians, which would have destroyed his bride, the noble Mordecai, whom he had earlier publicly honored, and many other good and innocent people.

I am sure the king wondered how he could have been so foolish as to have trusted Haman and not thought for himself. Haman was evil. It is possible the king realized that Haman may have had designs on becoming king himself, and now this evil man was eating with the king and queen! The king was angry at himself and furious with Haman.

The king had to get away for a few minutes to clear his mind. Leaving the table, he hastily stormed out into the palace garden to get a breath of fresh air and to clear his head while he considered his next plan of action. Haman was going to be fired, that was for sure. After

Haman was dismissed, then he would be able to think more clearly. He would get advice from the seven princes who had wisely counseled him many times before. With that in mind, he returned to the banquet.

While the king had excused himself, Haman realized that his well-thought-out plan had backfired. Haman had fallen on the queen's couch to plead for his life, knowing the king's rage was directed toward him, and more than just his cushy job was on the line.

When the king returned from the palace garden and saw Haman prostrate on his wife's couch—saw her fear and revulsion as she froze in terror at the nearness of the wicked man—the king exploded in anger. Along with all Haman had already done, now it seemed he was attempting to rape the queen.

Misinterpreting Haman's posturing, the king ordered his immediate execution. Faithful servants immediately hurried to cover Haman's face. Earlier that day, Haman's head covered in shame was an ironic foreshadowing of having his face covered prior to his execution.

The news of Haman's brand-new gallows and its intended use had already reached the ears of the royal chamberlain, Harbonah. The faithful servant, bravely facing the furious king, wasted no time in pointing out this fact to the king, emphasizing that Haman had intended the gallows to be used to execute faithful Mordecai.

HARBONAH SPEAKS: *"Maybe I was jealous, but I could see Haman was pure evil. Since Haman came into the picture, the king had rejected the wise counsel of those who had been with him for years in favor of this disagreeable person. I knew Haman wanted to be king and was angling his way there, but the king was oblivious to that. I heard about the gallows and the plan for the murder of Mordecai. When the king ordered Haman's execution, I was only too happy to inform him about Haman's new gallows, as it will now be put to good use."*

TIPS ON PLEASING THE KING: The final straw came when the king perceived the safety of his queen was threatened. Although he had misinterpreted Haman's final actions, the safety of his bride was of utmost importance. This is a picture of the love Christ has for His bride, His church—all those who have accepted Him as their personal Savior. Just as the king loved Esther and was going to do all he could to protect her and her people, so, too, does Christ love His church.

Christ proved His love by giving His life for all mankind, making the way to heaven open for believers. Since He did such a thing for His people, we know He cares about their day-to-day activities. Let me encourage you, during your trials and troubles, to look at the big picture. Remember the love God has for you in providing the way to save your eternal soul from hell. God let His Son be sacrificed for you so you can be with Him for eternity.

When you focus on the large picture, the one that includes eternity, you begin to realize the great love God has for us. I believe that in our flesh we cannot ever fully comprehend it. Even through the trials of this life, God loves us and He will bring us through. When this life is over, we have the assurance of heaven with Him Who died for us, rose again, and intercedes to the Father for us.

God protects us. The ultimate protection He gives us is the security and the certainty of heaven. No matter what happens in this life, the fact is that for the believer, "being absent from the body is to be present with the Lord" (2 Corinthians 5:8). It is God's responsibility to take care of His people while they are in this present, sin-cursed world; and when this life ends, there is a transition to the very presence of God in heaven, where no evil can ever enter or disturb us again.

The believer is securely held in the strong hands of God. The promise of God is everlasting life. Since God has promised this to His people, then He has promised everlasting protection. Take time today to thank God for His wonderful protection through the trials of this life. The same God Who provides the protection of heaven will protect you in the world He controls today.

Words from Our King

Thus saith the LORD of hosts; After the glory hath he sent me unto the nations which spoiled you: for he that toucheth you toucheth the apple of his eye.
(Zachariah 2:8)

My beloved is mine, and I am his.
(Song of Solomon 2:16)

As the Father knoweth me, even so know I the Father: and I lay down my life for the sheep. (John 10:15)

Who shall separate us from the love of Christ? shall tribulation, or distress, or persecution, or famine, or nakedness, or peril, or sword? (Romans 8:35)

In this was manifested the love of God toward us, because that God sent his only begotten Son into the world, that we might live through him. (1 John 4:9)

DAY 23

Haman Executed

BIBLE LESSON: The king's order to hang Haman on the gallows Hama had built for Mordecai was immediately carried out, as we read in today's verse. The enemy had to be removed and completely destroyed. According to history, a condemned person like Haman would be put to death publicly. And even after death, his body would be raised in view to a great height, making him both an example and a warning to all of the king's subjects. The king, not Haman, was in control of his subjects, and the king would not tolerate evildoers.

The gallows Haman had prepared was 50 cubits or approximately 90 feet high (Bible scholars disagree on the actual length of a cubit). It was not a gallows with a hanging rope to strangle the condemned but rather a sharpened pole upon which the condemned would be impaled. The great height was to advertise the death, making sure no one in the city was exempt from seeing this gruesome display.

For the Jews and the others who were affected by the wickedness of Haman, this public execution was a show of triumph, a cause for celebration that justice finally did triumph, and a fact that the evil one had been destroyed.

THE KING SPEAKS: *"I could not believe it! Haman, the man I trusted so implicitly, my main advisor, was all this time plotting against my noble, beautiful, and honorable queen and her people! And my wonderful one was eating twice with that deplorable enemy at our table. I am glad he already had the gallows built; it saved me time."*

TIPS ON PLEASING THE KING: Haman is a type of our enemy, the Devil. In his jealous rage against God, he deceived Eve in the garden of Eden; and he is still working his wiles today in seeking our death and destruction. 1 Peter 5:8 refers to Satan as "your adversary the devil, as a roaring lion, walketh about, seeking whom he may devour."

Just as the faithful Harbonah suggested Haman's punishment, so, too, Christians probably will have a part in the judgment of Satan. Paul reminds us in 1 Corinthians 6:3, "Know ye not that we shall judge angels?" Satan is an angel, albeit a fallen one. God may ask us to weigh in on the final punishment of Satan himself. And as Esther's king justly and finally dispatched the enemy, so, too, will Christ eliminate Satan forever. At the end of time as we know it, and before Christ can bring in the new heaven and the new earth, He must first put away sin. God does so by casting Satan into the lake of fire, where he will be tormented for all eternity. This precious promise is found in Revelation 20:10: "And the devil that deceived them was cast into the lake of fire and brimstone, where the beast and the false prophet are, and shall be tormented day and night forever and ever."

This verse is written in past tense to show us that God said it, planned it, purposed it, wrote it in His book, and showed this to His servant John. This action is as certain as if it had been already accomplished. Just as the execution of the evil Haman was a public display, so will be that of Satan (Isaiah 14:16). Then, and only then, will Christ's righteous anger and, may I add, all the people's sufferings—in whatever way by the works and the deceptions of the Devil—finally be appeased.

The Bible records in Philippians 2:11 that "every knee will bow, and every tongue confess that Jesus Christ is Lord." In a world where God is mocked and evil seems to triumph over good so many times, it's encouraging to know a time will come when all those who have mocked God will bow their knee and confess the lordship of our Savior, Christ Jesus. Like Haman, they will not prevail; they will be helpless in the presence of a far greater power than any earthly monarch. They will be forced to kneel before God and submit to His righteous judgment, after they use their God-given tongue to acknowledge the lordship of Jesus Christ. This will happen before they will be taken to their final and eternal judgment in the lake of fire (Revelation 20:15).

Keep in mind, as a Christian, that whoever is troubling you today is troubling God too. Thank God that He gives everyone the opportunity while they live to willingly come to Him, kneel in repentance, and receive His free gift of eternal life. Thank Him for His eventual justice for all those who are willingly being used by the Devil to persecute you. Thank God for His righteous judgments and His justice, for there is coming a day when we will enjoy the satisfaction of righteous justice having been done.

On another note, just as Haman was totally dispatched by the word of the king, so, too, will another enemy be one day destroyed. That enemy is death, itself. Death is an enemy who takes the precious gift of life away from our loved ones, and eventually ourselves. As Christians, we do everything we can to make sure that both ourselves and our loved ones avoid this enemy for as long as possible. Nevertheless, in this life, that enemy does prevail. But with every death and every impending death we face, we can be reminded of the precious promise found in 1 Corinthians 15:26: "The last enemy that shall be destroyed is death." One day, death itself finally will be destroyed.

Words from Our King

Render unto our neighbours sevenfold into their bosom
their reproach, wherewith they have reproached thee,
O Lord. (Psalm 79:12)

The wicked in his pride doth persecute the poor: let
them be taken in the devices that they have imagined.
(Psalm 10:2)

The righteousness of the perfect shall direct his way:
but the wicked shall fall by his own wickedness.
(Proverbs 11:5)

How art thou fallen from heaven, O Lucifer, son of the
morning! how art thou cut down to the ground, which
didst weaken the nations! (Isaiah 14:12)

He will swallow up death in victory; and the Lord GOD
will wipe away tears from off all faces; and the rebuke
of his people shall he take away from off all the earth:
for the LORD hath spoken it. (Isaiah 25:8)

DAY 24

Esther's Tears

BIBLE READING: ESTHER 8:1–14

BIBLE LESSON: Esther 8 ushers in a new beginning for the king, for Esther, for Mordecai, and for all the Jews in the province.

With Haman dead, his office was now empty. It appears that on Haman's death, the king also seized all of Haman's property and gave it to Esther. The king quickly realized Mordecai, the Jew, would make an excellent second-in-command, and promoted him to Haman's former position. The king also gave Mordecai his signet ring as a symbol of the authority of his new office. Esther then immediately passed on the estate of Haman to Mordecai. Mordecai literally went from rags to riches within hours.

The king had promised Esther that whatever her petition was, he would grant it, even to half of the kingdom. Three times in two days, he repeated his kind and sincere words of promise to her. She had yet to ask him for anything more than two dinner invitations.

Since the law for the destruction of the Jews was passed, Queen Esther appeared emotionally strong and was holding up quite well. She had fasted; she had prepared and followed through with not one, but two banquets; and in the meantime, she had entertained the king in a royal way. Because of her actions, Haman was executed and Mordecai exalted. But in verse 3 of chapter 8, all of the stress seems to catch up with her, and she collapses in tears before the king, begging him to reconsider the law that would destroy the Jews.

Esther, weeping before the king, specifically asked that the law he had signed under the advice of Haman be reversed. But according to the law of the Medes and Persians, any decree signed by the king could not be changed, and Mordecai and the king both knew this. The king was at a loss as to just how to keep his promise to Esther and to undo his unwise decision. Perhaps on the advice of Mordecai, he decided to amend the existing law.

Mordecai changed Haman's original decree, adding that the Jews not only had the right to defend themselves aggressively, but also gave them the authority to take the offensive and kill all those who would seek their hurt. The day Haman had originally decreed for the Jews' mass destruction was turned so that now the Jews had the upper hand.

MORDECAI SPEAKS: *"This is more than I could have ever dreamed about. I simply wanted myself and my people spared from mass destruction. I realized Jehovah*

allowed Hadassah to become queen for a reason. All I
could think was that she was there to save our people.
Now I have been promoted second to the king, Haman is
dead, and I have all of his wealth and property. The law
will be changed so that our people will be spared. I
remember a verse from the Psalms that says, 'Weeping
may endure for a night, but joy cometh in the morning.'
Truly, Jehovah has heard our prayers and turned our
tears into joy."

TIPS ON PLEASING THE KING: Ladies, it is okay to
cry; Esther shows us this. She had accomplished much,
yet wanted, yes, even needed, so much more. She was
still far from saving all of her people. Although
Haman's death and Mordecai's promotion were a great
and unexpected blessing, this was not what she wanted.
The lives of her people were still very much in danger,
even though both her life and Mordecai's were safe.
Esther was going to ask and keep asking until she got
what she wanted—until her mission was accomplished.

Esther is similar to another woman in the Bible, Caleb's
daughter. Caleb gave his daughter a gift of land, and
although she was appreciative and grateful, she wanted
more; she wanted the springs of water too. Perhaps she
needed the extra water to make her land fruitful. Her
request to her father and his answer are recorded in
Joshua 15:19: "Give me a blessing; for thou hast given
me a south land; give me also springs of water. And he
gave her the upper springs, and the nether springs."

Like Esther, Caleb's daughter wanted more to complement her original blessing.

Perhaps this devotional is coming to you at a time when you are begging God for something, and still you do not have His answer. As you continue to cry out to Him, He is moving people, arranging circumstances, and working behind the scenes to bring you not only your answer, but also greater things than you can imagine. But until then, let me encourage you to both thank and praise God for all of His blessings, for His goodness, and for His workings, even when you haven't "seen" them. Continue to ask for what you desperately want. You may be praying for a loved one to get saved, a marriage to be restored, a wayward child to return, wisdom and direction in your daily life, and so on. Do not be afraid to be like Esther, and ask God for these spiritual blessings, even with tears. God hears your prayers and sees your need, and He will provide. Jesus Himself taught His disciples to ask and to keep asking in prayer to God for what they wanted or needed. Sometimes, God wants to see how bad we want something before He gives it to us. So be like Esther, and don't settle for only half a blessing when you need or even want more. Keep asking God for what you want; it is known as importunity.

Words from Our King

Ask of me, and I shall give thee the heathen for thine inheritance, and the uttermost parts of the earth for thy possession. (Psalm 2:8)

Thou hast delivered my soul from death, mine eyes from tears, and my feet from falling. (Psalm 116:8)

When it goeth well with the righteous, the city rejoiceth: and when the wicked perish, there is shouting. (Proverbs 11:10)

A good man leaveth an inheritance to his children's children: and the wealth of the sinner is laid up for the just. (Proverbs 13:22)

I say unto you, Ask, and it shall be given you; seek, and ye shall find; knock, and it shall be opened unto you. For every one that asketh receiveth; and he that seeketh findeth; and to him that knocketh it shall be opened. (Luke 11:9–10)

DAY 25

Mordecai Reigns

BIBLE READING: ESTHER 8:15–17

BIBLE LESSON: The wise Mordecai was well fitted for Haman's old position. Not long before, Mordecai was arrayed in royal finery and paraded through town, honored by the king for a few hours. Now, Mordecai was officially in the position of second-in-command, with all of the rights of that position. The royal garments were now truly his—not borrowed temporarily from the king.

Because of Mordecai's advancement, the entire city of Shushan rejoiced because there was a good man in command. More likely than not, the king's seven counselors welcomed Mordecai, knowing he had the king's best interests at heart.

The new, amended decree giving the Jews the right to defend themselves was met with rejoicing. Not only were they going to be spared, they also were given, by law, the right to destroy their oppressors. This good news turned their fear into joy and their fasting into feasting.

Not only did the Jews rejoice, but many other people of different ethnic and religious backgrounds accepted both the religion and the God of the Jews. The Bible records their reasoning in these words: "for the fear of the Jews fell upon them" (v. 17). Perhaps those who converted to Judaism were not only afraid of the Jews, but also realized what a great salvation their God had provided in sparing all of His people. They, too, wanted the protection of the God of the Jews.

A JEW SPEAKS: *"Only recently, Mordecai was honored by the king and was led around by that wicked Haman. He certainly deserved that honor, and more. Now Mordecai is officially exalted, and we are so happy. He is a wise and good man—and fears Jehovah. We are truly blessed to have this humble man to rule over us. Now my wife is preparing a feast for both our family and also for our non-Jewish friends to celebrate Jehovah's deliverance."*

TIPS ON PLEASING THE KING: One of the lessons learned from this account is that of our responsibility and our privilege to pray for those in authority. Although it is not recorded, I believe Mordecai was faithful in his prayers for his king long before Esther became queen. His prayers for the king and his advisors (including Haman too!) no doubt continued after Esther was taken to the palace.

Some have said it is both our duty and responsibility as citizens to vote. While I certainly agree with this statement, let me make a further comment and encourage you, as a Christian, not only to vote, but also to understand that praying for those in authority is an even greater duty and responsibility. Voting takes place occasionally, but prayers to God on behalf of our government should be a daily habit.

Human government is ordained by God. The leaders in our state and nation were not placed there by our votes alone. Rather, we are told in Daniel 4:17 "that the living may know that the most High ruleth in the kingdom of men, and giveth it to whomsoever he will, and setteth up over it the basest of men."

When Jesus was on trial before Pilate, and Pilate told Jesus he had the power to either crucify or release Him, Jesus said to Pilate, "Thou couldest have no power at all against me, except it were given thee from above:" (John 19:11). The power Pilate had against the Son of God to crucify Him was the authority God the Father gave to him, knowing Pilate would be used to try to kill the body of His Son.

Since it is God Who places our leaders in authority (and sometimes we see the "basest of men"—perhaps Pilate could be included in this designation—in high positions), we are told in 1 Timothy 2:2 to "pray for kings and all that are in authority." The reason for our prayers is "so that we may lead a quiet and peaceable life in all godliness and honesty."

The passage in 1 Timothy 2:2 records that praying for those in authority is pleasing to God because He wants all men, even corrupt government leaders, to receive

Christ as their Savior. According to this passage, the focus of our prayers for those in authority should be for their salvation. What is interesting is that when Paul wrote to Timothy and exhorted him to pray for political leaders, it was a time when the Roman Emperor Nero—who was a corrupt leader—reigned and persecuted Christians. The apostle Paul was put to death during his reign.

While at times it may seem our prayers for those in authority are not answered, still the responsibility is on us to pray but the results are in God's hands. Whatever happens in our government, let us be found faithful in praying for those God has placed in authority. Someday, we will have our rewards and see the results of how God used our obedience to His command in ways we cannot know now.

Let me encourage you today to start a new habit: praying for government leaders in your town, state, and country. Ask God to give them wisdom to do their jobs, wisdom for their counseling, and most of all, assurance of salvation for them and their loved ones. You will be obeying God, which will bring blessings perhaps far greater than you can even think or imagine.

Words from Our King

All the ends of the world shall remember and turn unto the LORD: and all the kindreds of the nations shall worship before thee. (Psalm 22:27)

The kingdom is the LORD'S: and he is the governor among the nations. (Psalm 22:28)

When the righteous are in authority, the people rejoice: but when the wicked beareth rule, the people mourn. (Proverbs 29:2)

Seek the peace of the city whither I have caused you to be carried away captives, and pray unto the LORD for it: for in the peace thereof shall ye have peace. (Jeremiah 29:7)

I exhort therefore, that, first of all, supplications, prayers, intercessions, and giving of thanks, be made for all men; For kings, and for all that are in authority; that we may lead a quiet and peaceable life in all godliness and honesty. (1Timothy 2:1–2)

DAY 26

Slaughter and Rejoicing

BIBLE READING: ESTHER CHAPTER 9:1–6

BIBLE LESSON: The date is the thirteenth of Adar. According to the Hebrew calendar, Adar is a winter month consisting of twenty-nine days. Although the Persians were in power at that time, the Jews evidently used the Hebrew calendar.

After casting a lot (what the Persians called "Pur"), this was the day Haman had determined would be the best day for the destruction of the Jews. But now, Mordecai, the Jew, was in authority, and the situation was reversed—the hunted were now the hunters. The law Haman devised had been amended so that the Jews would have the power to kill their enemies on this day.

The authority Mordecai wielded was not taken lightly. Mordecai was feared and became ruler over all local authorities. Anyone who dared to go against his laws was either dismissed from his position and replaced, or executed. Everyone who took up arms against the Jews in the Persian empire were destroyed on the thirteenth of Adar.

The Bible records that in Shushan, in the palace alone, the Jews killed five hundred men. There may have been women and children killed, but they were not counted. The interesting fact is that no one had to die—all these deaths were needless. Those who hated the Jews could have put their hatred aside and respected the Jews as fellow human beings. Those who were killed died because of their own hard hearts.

A RULER OF THE PROVINCE SPEAKS: *"I never disliked the Jewish people; but some of the other rulers did, and tried to make their lives miserable just because they were Jews. Mordecai made sure that those who hated the Jews were quickly removed from positions of authority, or they were killed. I wanted to keep my position, so I made special provision for all the Jews in my province. In the days leading up to Adar 13, I made sure everyone knew I was going to help the Jews against those who hated them. Some of the rulers lost their lives when the Jews rose up, but because of my precautions and respect for Mordecai, I am still the ruler of my province, and I am still alive."*

TIPS ON PLEASING THE KING: The Bible says "it is a fearful thing to fall into the hands of the living God" (Hebrews 10:31). While reading this verse, please note that the Bible does not say it is a fearful thing to cast oneself into the hands of the living God.

We see both, fall versus cast oneself, in this passage from Esther. Mordecai is an illustration of God. Mordecai was feared and respected. Those who hardened their hearts against the command of Mordecai were executed. That was a fearful thing. However, those who were willing to obey Mordecai, take his orders, follow them, and help the Jews did not have to fear Mordecai's wrath.

What is very interesting to note in this passage is that all non-Jews had a choice, and everyone made a choice. They could have hardened their hearts against Mordecai and been destroyed—that was a choice. Or they could have obeyed the rule of Mordecai, helped the Jews, and lived; and that was a choice.

The king's commandment had been announced several months earlier. All those in Shushan knew that on a certain day, they were either going to rebel against the Jews—and possibly lose their lives trying—or they would yield to the king by obeying Mordecai and by helping the Jews.

Today, things are similar. Each of us has been given a precious gift call "time." Along with this precious gift is a choice of life or death. While physical death will happen to all of us (Hebrews 9:27 tells us "it is appointed unto men once to die, but after this the judgment"), what we do during our lifetime will determine our judgment after we pass from this physical world. We get to choose for ourselves eternal life or eternal death.

Those who put themselves, or willingly cast themselves, into the hands of the living God find, like those in Mordecai's day, both life and freedom and favorable judgment after physical death. Those who harden their hearts are physically destroyed when they choose death.

For those of us who choose life, we are still under the rule of God. Another life lesson we can learn from this passage of Scripture about the massacre of those who hated the Jews is that once we have chosen life—and God—we must make a thorough cleansing of sin in our lives.

As Christians, we can harden our hearts when it comes to our pet sins; and I believe we all have some sort of favorite sin issue we don't want to deal with. However, hardening our hearts and keeping that sin will destroy our service to God in some way. Let me encourage you as a Christian woman to search your heart on a regular basis and remove the sin that you find there (Hebrews 12:1). When you willingly put yourself into the hands of the living God, you will find life and life more abundant.

The more you strive to live your life to please God, by dealing with personal sin, the closer you will get to God—and the more you will enjoy Him. Just as there was a wonderful change in the city of Shushan after all those who hated the Jews were put away, you, too, can have a wonderful change after you make an honest and conscious effort to put away sin in your life for the glory of God. Submit yourself to the command of God in every area of your life; you will not be sorry.

Words from Our King

I call heaven and earth to record this day against you, that I have set before you life and death, blessing and cursing: therefore choose life, that both thou and thy seed may live: (Deuteronomy 30:19)

The fear of the LORD is a fountain of life, to depart from the snares of death. (Proverbs 14:27)

Verily, verily, I say unto you, He that heareth my word, and believeth on him that sent me, hath everlasting life, and shall not come into condemnation; but is passed from death unto life. (John 5:24)

To be carnally minded is death; but to be spiritually minded is life and peace. (Romans 8:6)

Rulers are not a terror to good works, but to the evil. Wilt thou then not be afraid of the power? do that which is good, and thou shalt have praise of the same. (Romans 13:3)

DAY 27

Second (and Last) Day of Slaughter

BIBLE READING: ESTHER 9:7–19

BIBLE LESSON: A single day of slaughter of the enemies of the Jews was not enough as there were more enemies that had to be destroyed. The day before, the Jews killed 75,000 enemies; and Queen Esther requested that the destruction of the Jews' enemies continue the next day also, on Adar 14, but this time only in the palace area. The Jews killed three hundred more of their enemies, bringing the total of all persons killed to 75,800.

While the killing and destruction of the enemies of the Jews continued, none of the Jews took any of the possessions of their enemies. The point of this mass destruction was not to loot their neighbors' goods, but to totally erase, from history and from memory, those who dared to put their hand against Jehovah's chosen ones.

An interesting request made by Queen Ester was that the dead bodies of Haman's ten sons were to be publicly displayed for everyone to see. While this was an unusual request and Esther's intent is not known, this public display of Haman's dead sons showed nothing was hidden, none of his seed had escaped. Justice had been served.

After the two days of killing were over, the Jews held a great celebration. The Jews at the palace in Shushan did not enjoy this day of rejoicing until Adar 15. The palace had to be purged more carefully and thoroughly than any other place in the kingdom.

There was rest after these two days of bloodshed, and the rest was made sweeter because the Jews no longer had fear of anyone. The non-Jews who survived were their friends and helpers, and some of them had even converted to the Jewish religion.

The Bible says the day after was a good day. There were no regrets about what had happened yesterday. The bloodshed was justifiable warfare, and now there was rejoicing and gladness. The enemy was put away, and now the Jews and their friends could live without fear. Exotic and expensive dishes were cooked, and gifts and food were given to the poor so that no one was left out of this wonderful celebration.

A JEWISH LADY SPEAKS: *"My husband came home today totally exhausted but jubilant. Finally, the slaughter is finished. The display of the bodies of Haman's ten sons, although a gruesome display, is*

*satisfying because justice has been served. Nothing
concerning Haman will attempt to wipe out our people
ever again. Our rejoicing tomorrow will be fuller and
more satisfying knowing we now can live our lives in
peace."*

TIPS ON PLEASING THE KING: The closer you are to
the king, i.e., nearer the palace, the greater your
responsibility and degree of cleansing your heart and
life of sin. The Jews in the palace area had more work
to do than those in the outlying provinces—two days of
slaughter rather than one. The queen requested a
second day of slaughter of the Jews' enemies in the
palace area to eliminate all those who had escaped the
day before.

The closer we want to be to God (in our illustration,
those in the palace area), the more we have to clean up
our lives from worldly things that draw us away from
fellowship with God. Sometimes we need a thorough
cleansing of our sinful lives.

Haman's ten sons were made a public display to show
justice was finished. While it was against the law of
God to put these children to death for the sins of their
father, most likely, these ten, no matter how young or
old, had followed in the steps of their father's hatred of
the Jews. This public showing the day after they died
convinced the Jews that these were people who were
cursed of God Himself. God said specifically in
Deuteronomy 21:23 "he that is hanged is accursed of
God." The bodies of these men, impaled upon wooden

spikes for all the world to see, demonstrated to the Jewish people that justice had been accomplished. This was a satisfaction to all Jews who had suffered and feared under the rule of Haman.

This is also a picture of Jesus. He became sin because He took on Himself the punishment of our sins. He who was totally innocent, Who came only to do good, and Who always did the will of the Father, became a curse to His Father, God. This was so when He hung upon the tree of Calvary and paid the price for the sins of the whole world. But most importantly, Jesus's death was special for God the Father, showing Him justice was completely served. The payment for sin was paid in full, and the Father was satisfied. The Son's words were simply, "It is finished" (John 19:30).

After this cleansing of the palace, and ultimately of the kingdom, there was rejoicing. The rejoicing could not have come so long as there were still the effects of sin; sin had to be eliminated before there could be rejoicing.

This is a fact in our lives today. As Christians, we have daily cleansing from sin, confession, and repenting and forsaking sin and its pleasures. Then there is rejoicing as we ask Christ to clean up our hearts and lives with His precious blood.

In Esther's day, the Jews finally had rest from their enemies. In this life, we are on guard against the sin in our lives and around us. The battle is never quite finished. We do get times of rest and rejoicing when we confess and forsake our sins, but as long as we are in the flesh, we will never be completely free of sin. Our final rest and eternal rejoicing will come when we are finally and totally delivered from the effects of sin, and our fleshy bodies are transformed into glorified ones. For the Christian, this will be an even better day than what the Jews experienced as a "good day" in Esther's time.

Words from Our King

His body shall not remain all night upon the tree, but thou shalt in any wise bury him that day; (for he that is hanged is accursed of God;) that thy land be not defiled, which the LORD thy God giveth thee for an inheritance. (Deuteronomy 21:23)

The LORD loveth judgment, and forsaketh not his saints; they are preserved for ever: but the seed of the wicked shall be cut off. (Psalm 37:28)

He said unto them, Go your way, eat the fat, and drink the sweet, and send portions unto them for whom nothing is prepared: for this day is holy unto our Lord: neither be ye sorry; for the joy of the LORD is your strength. (Nehemiah 8:10)

There remaineth therefore a rest to the people of God. (Hebrews 4:9)

When he ascended up on high, he led captivity captive,
and gave gifts unto men. (Ephesians 4:8)

DAY 28

Feast of Purim

BIBLE READING: ESTHER 9: 15–32

BIBLE LESSON: Haman cast a lot (like drawing numbers out of a hat) to determine the best "lucky" days to destroy the Jews. God turned that plan into destruction for both Haman and other people who hated the Jews.

Things changed around the palace and province. The Jews did not live in fear of enemies, and they received new respect from their neighbors. Therefore, the day was set aside as a yearly holiday so it would be remembered and celebrated.

Mordecai wrote proclamations to all the king's provinces to make the fourteenth and fifteenth days of the month of Adar a national holiday—to remember the victory God gave to His people—and he named this holiday "Purim," after Pur, the lottery used to pick that particular day.

To this day, the feast of Purim is still celebrated by Jewish people as a holiday of celebrating, remembering, and rejoicing in Jehovah's goodness. Usually, it lasts for two days, during the month of February or March.

A JEW SPEAKS: *"I am so glad Mordecai and Queen Esther established the feast of Purim. Our people must always remember this wonderful event, when we were miraculously delivered from certain destruction and instead were able to defeat those who hated us. For the first time in many years, we now have complete rest and total victory from our enemies. To Jehovah be the glory!"*

TIPS ON PLEASING THE KING: While the Jews celebrate Purim, you may ask: "Should Christians celebrate Purim?" When we read this account in Esther, we feel joyful about what God did for His people. However, the feast of Purim is a Jewish holiday and not one that needs to be celebrated by Christians today.

But in a sense, Christians should (and most do) participate in a type of observance or remembrance. In fact, there are at least five different instances when we, as Christians, should remember the past. These are:

Baptism—This is a public event and an outward testimony of our salvation. When we follow the Lord in believer's baptism, we remember our salvation, which was usually a private act that occurred sometime in our past. At our baptism, we remember when we got saved, and we publicly share our testimony with others.

Communion—During the communion service, we remember the death of Jesus on the cross. We reflect on all He has done for us, by paying the price for our sins.

He asks us to look back and remember His death and His broken body, as recorded in the Gospels. This is a solemn time of remembrance and obedience on our part, which we cannot take lightly. He did all the work for us, and now He asks us to look back in remembrance. We will never fully realize the extent of the pain and agony He suffered before and on the cross because of His love for us; but we can and should remember what He did for us during the communion service.

Christmas and Easter—These two holidays, held dear by Christians everywhere, bring to mind at Christmastime the first gift of the physical body of Jesus to the world; and during the Easter season, the remembrance of Jesus Christ's physical death, burial, and body. There could be no Easter without Christmas. And without the triumphant resurrection of Christ from the dead, we would have no hope of our salvation, let alone our bodily resurrection.

Past blessings—Remembering God's answers to our past prayers encourages us and is also a way of praising Him in the present. You may have your own personal Purim about when God miraculously delivered you from a terrible fate. That is a good thing to remember. The blessings and answered prayers God gave you in the past are both a reminder and an encouragement for you to take into your present difficulties. When you look back over all God has done for you, know He has not brought you so far just to fail. God has helped you through past trials and blessed you, and He will continue to help you, both today and until you meet Him face-to-face.

The look backward is just that—a look. We cannot allow ourselves to rest on our laurels and be content with what we have allowed God to do in our lives already. If you are reading this devotional, you can be sure God has something He still wants you to do for Him. Use the past to better yourself in both the present and the future.

While there is a time for us to look backward in time and remember what God did for us personally and then take that memory into our future, there are also some things in our past we should forget. We all have committed sins and experienced some sort of failure. The trite phrase that hindsight is 20-20 means that after something did not go right, we realized what we should have done or said. However, to dwell on long ago shortcomings is both pointless and defeating. When your heart is dwelling in the past, you, like Lot's wife, become useless.

The past is gone; learn from your mistakes. But do not allow those mistakes and failures to define or to rob your present or future. The apostle Paul, in Philippians 3:13, implores us to follow his example in "forgetting those things which are behind and reaching forth unto those things which are before." This concept of forgetting what is behind applies to both our failures and our triumphs. After a glance backward, go forward into the future, better armed with what you know now so you can better serve God.

Words from Our King

Thou hast turned for me my mourning into dancing: thou hast put off my sackcloth and girded me with gladness. (Psalm 30:11)

I will remember the works of the LORD: surely I will remember thy wonders of old. (Psalm 77:11)

Remember his marvellous works that he hath done; his wonders, and the judgments of his mouth. (Psalm 105:5)

Remember the former things of old: for I am God, and there is none else; I am God, and there is none like me. (Isaiah 46:9)

To appoint unto them that mourn in Zion, to give unto them beauty for ashes, the oil of joy for mourning, the garment of praise for the spirit of heaviness; that they might be called trees of righteousness, the planting of the LORD, that he might be glorified. (Isaiah 61:3)

DAY 29

Mordecai the Jew

BIBLE READING: ESTHER CHAPTER 10:1–3

BIBLE LESSON: The book of Esther ends with chapter 10, which is a mere three verses containing only ninety-three words. This last chapter has a very satisfactory "happily ever after" feel that concludes this remarkable narrative. Yet within this very short chapter, Esther is not even mentioned. The central figure is Mordecai. Mordecai emerged as a strong, revered, historical, and political figure, who concealed neither his religious heritage nor his nationality. This wise, peaceful, and quiet Jew who sat at the king's gate had risen to be second-in-command of the king's provinces—very similar to Joseph in the Book of Genesis. The king now seemed to be a figurehead and Mordecai the actual ruler of the realm. Mordecai had set the example of a good leader, using his elevated position to accomplish much good for his people.

Also, the Jews and King Ahasuerus increased their wealth after Mordecai got his promotion because Mordecai looked after the financial interests of both.

King Ahasuerus successfully taxed both his land and the islands he controlled. God's blessing on this heathen Persian king was a direct result of the promise God gave to Abram in Genesis 12:3 concerning the future Jewish race, when He said, "And I will bless them that bless thee, and curse him that curseth thee."

Mordecai was a good man, in that he feared and trusted God and did his duty, as a loyal and honest citizen, toward the king. As such, he was an instrument used by God to bring great prosperity to the Jews throughout the Persian empire. While the Bible is silent on the rest of the life of Esther, Mordecai, and King Ahasuerus, the last three words of the book of Esther—"all his seed"—may hint that Esther and the king had children. The blessing Esther and Mordecai brought to the land lasted for generations.

THE KING SPEAKS: *"I am so blessed. My chief advisor, my loyal subject, is not only my friend but also my father-in-law. I have a queen who loves me, and the man who raised her is also my trusted second-in-command. I know I can safely trust Mordecai because I know I can trust Esther's heart."*

TIPS ON PLEASING THE KING: Consider the phrase "Mordecai the Jew." There is much in these three words and a lesson for us Christians. There is a special reference given to Mordecai as a Jew in this passage of Scripture. Mordecai did not hide his ethnicity, nor was he ashamed of what being a Jew meant. Being a Jew in Mordecai's time was being a part of a minority, with not only a cultural reference but also a religious designation.

When people think about you, are you easily linked with the designation of "Christian?" The term "Christian" literally means "little Christs," which informs us that we need to emulate Christ. Or do you hide your affiliation and prefer to be a secret-agent Christian? I am not saying you should be an "in-your-face-everyone-is-going-to-hell" type of Christian, which would turn people away from hearing the gospel message. But following Christ as a public testimony, and not being afraid or ashamed to be labeled as a Christian, is to be aware of how your deeds and your words reflect on your status as a Christian. Some actions to consider are: being unashamed of praying in public; sincerely telling people you are/will pray for them; doing your tasks faithfully in service to the Lord; being unashamed of your church attendance; and being seen holding a Bible—in public. Other ways of promoting your Christian testimony is in not joining in on ungodly topics of conversation; striving to have clean and edifying language; and being ready to answer any question that may be asked about your faith.

Perhaps you don't want to be known as a Christian because you are afraid that if you mess up, your testimony will be marred. Unfortunately, we do not always behave like little Christs. God does not expect us to be sinless, but as Christians, we do need to sin less. It is better to strive to have a clear Christian testimony and, perhaps, even with the best of intentions, to mess up at times, than to hide behind the flimsy excuse of fear of failure as a Christian, and not share our faith and our Savior at all. When you are only known to God as a Christian and not to others, you risk being ashamed of your Savior. It is your responsibility (and it is a great blessing) as a Christian to share the gospel with others, as God opens up doors of opportunity.

Mordecai was an honorable man; and he was not ashamed of his nationality, his God, or his king. He faithfully served as a Jew. As a Christian, you, too, should faithfully serve God and others. When you have a good testimony for Jesus Christ and you desire to point others to Him, you can be like Mordecai and have "seed" also—spiritual fruit, spiritual offspring. As such, you will be responsible for others coming to know Christ as their Savior. Paul uses this illustration in 1 Corinthians 4:15 when he says to the Christians in Corinth, "for in Christ Jesus I have begotten you through the gospel." Your testimony and your witness for Jesus Christ are important because they are necessary for spiritual reproduction. And God wants all of His children to reproduce spiritually, for His honor and glory.

Words from Our King

Let your light so shine before men, that they may see your good works, and glorify your Father which is in heaven. (Matthew 5:16)

The disciples were called Christians first in Antioch. (Acts 11:26)

I am not ashamed of the gospel of Christ: for it is the power of God unto salvation to every one that believeth; to the Jew first, and also to the Greek. (Romans 1:16)

Having your conversation honest among the Gentiles: that, whereas they speak against you as evildoers, they may by your good works, which they shall behold, glorify God in the day of visitation. (1 Peter 2:12)

If any man suffer as a Christian, let him not be ashamed; but let him glorify God on this behalf. (1 Peter 4:16)

DAY 30

Your Legacy

BIBLE READING: GENESIS 12:1–3

BIBLE LESSON: The suggested Bible reading for today is a look back to the origin of what we know today as the Jewish race. God promised Abram (later, God changed his name to Abraham) that he would be the father of a great nation. Today, that nation is the Jews.

Had Esther not decided to intercede for her people, the Jews, we know the truth in Mordecai's statement: "Then shall there enlargement and deliverance arise to the Jews from another place" (Esther 4:14). Mordecai knew Jehovah would deliver His people, but he also believed Jehovah God had placed his young charge, Esther, in a very particular place to complete a great and necessary work. And because of that work, the Jewish race is still here. Esther left a legacy; and that was her role in helping to preserve the lives of her people—members of the great nation God promised to Abraham—at that particular time in history.

A MODERN-DAY JEWISH WOMAN SPEAKS: *"I have so much to be thankful for, not only for Esther's*

– 147 –

actions but also for God's protection over my race throughout the centuries. Some have said the Jews are proof of the existence of God. I am thrilled to know I am an ancestor of such a beautiful, brave, and heroic woman. She is certainly one of my role models."

TIPS ON PLEASING THE KING: You, like Esther, have been placed by God Himself at an important time and in an important place for a special purpose and a specific reason. I don't know you, and I certainly don't know your circumstances; but I do know God has a purpose and work for you to do, just like He did for Esther. You may not be called upon to save an entire race of people, but God has something He desires you to do.

Although we might focus on one particular event in Esther's later life, all that she did before was in preparation for what God created her to do. Esther had a choice. She could have shirked her role, but she chose to do otherwise. You, too, have a choice every day to do what God has given you to do where He has placed you. You also have the privilege and responsibility to leave a legacy.

Esther was born, she lived, and then she died; but she left a legacy. As a human, you have been created for the pleasure of the living God. As a Christian, you have aligned yourself with something far bigger and greater than yourself, which makes you special. You have a unique purpose in this world no one else can fulfill. Allow me to encourage you to ask God how you can best serve Him with the talents and abilities He has given you.

There is a saying that has been attributed to an early twentieth century missionary C. T. Studd: "Only one life, 'twill soon be past, only what's done for Christ will last." Esther's deeds are recorded in eternal writ. You have your mission, so let me encourage you to live all of your days and do all of your tasks as unto Christ. Had Esther not bowed her will to God's by way of the king, she would not have been chosen to deliver her people. Yet her obedience in her daily activities, even the mundane ones, toward her adopted father, her royal husband, and, ultimately, to God Himself, made her both a useful and ultimately celebrated vessel. Again, let me encourage you to do all your daily activities for Christ.

What kind of legacy will you leave? Take some time today and ponder not only Esther's legacy but the legacy you are creating. Ask God what He would have you do so that when you leave this world, what you leave behind will continue on, touching lives and changing hearts long after you are gone.

Words from Our King

By thee have I been holden up from the womb: thou art he that took me out of my mother's bowels: my praise shall be continually of thee. (Psalm 71:6)

Whatsoever thy hand findeth to do, do it with thy might. (Ecclesiastes 9:10)

I know the thoughts that I think toward you, saith the LORD, thoughts of peace, and not of evil, to give you an expected end. (Jeremiah 29:11)

He that had received five talents came and brought other five talents, saying, Lord, thou deliveredst unto me five talents: behold, I have gained beside them five talents more. (Matthew 25:20)

I beseech you therefore, brethren, by the mercies of God, that ye present your bodies a living sacrifice, holy, acceptable unto God, which is your reasonable service. (Romans 12:1)

Dear Friend

Dear friend, thank you for reading my book. It is a great honor to me that you have chosen to read what I have written. But before you go, I want to ask you a very personal question: Are you absolutely sure that when you die you are bound for heaven?

Many women call themselves "Christian" because they believe in God, Jesus, and even the Holy Spirit, and this is all very good. They may pray to Jesus too. But Jesus Himself addressed this when He said,

> Not every one that saith unto me, Lord, Lord, shall enter into the kingdom of heaven; but he that doeth the will of my Father which is in heaven. Many will say to me in that day, Lord, Lord, have we not prophesied in thy name? and in thy name have cast out devils? and in thy name done many wonderful works? And then will I profess unto them, I never knew you: depart from me, ye that work iniquity.
>
> —Matthew 7:21–23

Wow! These are very powerful and harsh words! Jesus is saying He will personally tell some people to depart from Him, to actually go into hell, even though while they were alive they prophesied in His name, cast out devils, and did many wonderful works. What they did may be more than what you've ever done or will ever do.

My desire, and even more importantly God's desire, for you is that you know for sure that when you do meet Jesus face-to-face, He will welcome you into His holy heaven forever instead of saying, "Depart from me, ye that work iniquity." If you have any doubts about this, I pray you would make sure of this now.

The Bible, God's Holy Word to mankind, records, "These things have I written unto you that believe on the name of the Son of God; that ye may know that ye have eternal life, and that ye may believe on the name of the Son of God" (1 John 5:13). You can know *now* that you are assured of Jesus welcoming you into heaven when you die. Jesus said, "Ye must be born again" (John 3:7). Since He has made being born again a requirement for both salvation and heaven, He also tells you how to become born again.

You must first realize that you are a sinner and that your sins have separated you from God. "All have sinned, and come short of the glory of God" (Romans 3:23). As a sinner, you are condemned to death. "The wages of sin is death" (Romans 6:23). We have all earned those wages! This death is not only physical death but even more seriously, spiritual death, which is eternal separation from God in hell. "It is appointed unto men once to die, but after this the judgement" (Hebrews 9:27). After you physically die, you will still be spiritually alive to be judged of God and to see if He deems you worthy to enter His heaven.

The certain news is that you cannot enter heaven as a sinful human being. The good news is that Jesus Himself took your punishment for sin and died on the cross in your place. "God commendeth [shows] His love toward us, in that, while we were yet sinners, Christ died for us" (Romans 5:8).

God also tells you to repent: "God ... commandeth all men everywhere to repent" (Acts 17:30). Repentance is a change of mind, which agrees with God that you are a sinner. Repentance also means you agree that Jesus died for your sins on the cross.

If you believe Jesus took your sins, died in your place, was buried, and then after three days and three nights rose from the dead, then you can truly call on the name of the Lord to be saved. Romans 10:14 promises us "whosoever shall call upon the name of the Lord shall be saved." God also recorded in His Holy Word that when the apostle Paul and his friend Silas were asked, "What must I do to be saved?" they replied, "Believe on the Lord Jesus Christ, and thou shalt be saved" (Acts 16:30–31).

If you have any doubts you are saved, or fear you would not be welcomed into heaven, you can pray right now to God, asking Him to save you. You can use this sample prayer:

Dear Jesus, I know I am a sinner. I believe, and I thank You for taking my sins on Yourself when You died on the cross. I believe You bled, died, and were buried, and three days later You were resurrected. All that You did so long ago was for me now. Please come into my heart and save me from hell. Thank You for Your forgiveness of my sins and Your gift of heaven and everlasting life.

If you prayed this prayer and sincerely and humbly meant it—you have called upon the name of the Lord Jesus Christ and believed on the Lord Jesus Christ—you are saved. You now have the assurance of going to heaven when you die. You made a very wise decision. The Bible tells us "that if thou shalt confess with thy mouth the Lord Jesus, and shalt believe in thine heart that God hath raised him from the dead, thou shalt be saved. For with the heart man believeth unto righteousness; and with the mouth confession is made unto salvation" (Romans 10:9–10).

This action cannot be undone. You are now a child of God, and His Holy Spirit is living within you. Do not be afraid to tell others about what you did. The same God Who saved you is ready and willing to save your family and friends so they, too, can be assured of heaven.

Sincerely,

Mary Jane Humes

Acknowledgments

I was first introduced to the story of Esther as a preteen at West Cameron Gospel Hall in West Cameron Township, Pennsylvania, by my Sunday school teacher, the Miss Gina Spotts. I still remember my inward groaning, thinking that studying a whole book in the Bible would result in a boring time! But much to my surprise and delight, she opened up the narrative of Esther to me in such an interesting fashion that I found myself actually enjoying her teaching.

Many years later, when I became a Sunday school teacher myself, I passed on the beauty of this book to my students at Victory Bible Church in Paxinos, Pennsylvania; and I am grateful for the privilege of teaching there. A special thanks goes to Emily, who upon learning what "beheaded" meant (in relation to what may have happened to Vashti) would cover her eyes and stifle a horrified squeal every time she heard the word. Thanks to Josiah, who soaked up everything I taught like sponge; and to Verna, who honored me as her personal Bible teacher for many years after her time in my class had ended.

Many thanks to Dr Charles Brown of Winter Haven, Florida, who made many excellent suggestions on my rough draft of this book. He bravely edited this work when it was a little more than notes, but his initial edits and suggestions made things so much clearer for me as I continued my work.

Many thanks to my wonderful husband, Joseph, who faithfully edited my words. He caught and deleted my repetitions and encouraged me to tighten up my ramblings, with the result that you will read a much better work. I could not have done this without his thoughtful insights.

And a special thanks to my mother, the late Dorothy Rhodes, who would listen to me ramble on, about the joy I had in starting to create this devotional, perhaps silently wondering if she would ever have the privilege of holding my finished work. She never did. The Lord took her to be with Him, which is far better than reading anything I could have written.

Lastly, but certainly not least, a huge amount of thanks to my wonderful and favorite uncle, Ralph Hornberger of Feasterville Trevose, Pennsylvania, who laboriously and painstakingly fine-tooth-combed the entire thirty chapters (days). His efforts have resulted in an excellent finished product which has his stamp of approval.

About the Author

Photo, hair, and makeup by Lindsey Hoke

Mary Jane Humes's desire to learn, coupled with a bit of adventure, led her into several various job positions, a few of which actually utilized her BA in biology. Raised on a steady diet of books but no TV, she always had a dream of writing a book someday, so she did. *Esther's Faith* is her second book. Currently she teaches Sunday School and plays the piano for her church.

When Mary Jane is not writing, she loves working on her property with her husband, Joseph, and caring for all of their rescued furry little ones.

CONTACT

LINKEDIN: www.linkedin.com/in/mary-jane-humes
FACEBOOK: www.facebook.com/mjhumes
EMAIL: hello@maryjanehumes.com
WEBSITE: maryjanehumes.com

Can You Help?

Reviews are everything to an author, because they mean a book is given more visibility. If you enjoyed this book, please review it on your favorite book review sites and tell your friends about it. Thank you!

Made in the USA
Monee, IL
27 June 2022